King and Miranda

**The Poetry
of the
Machine**

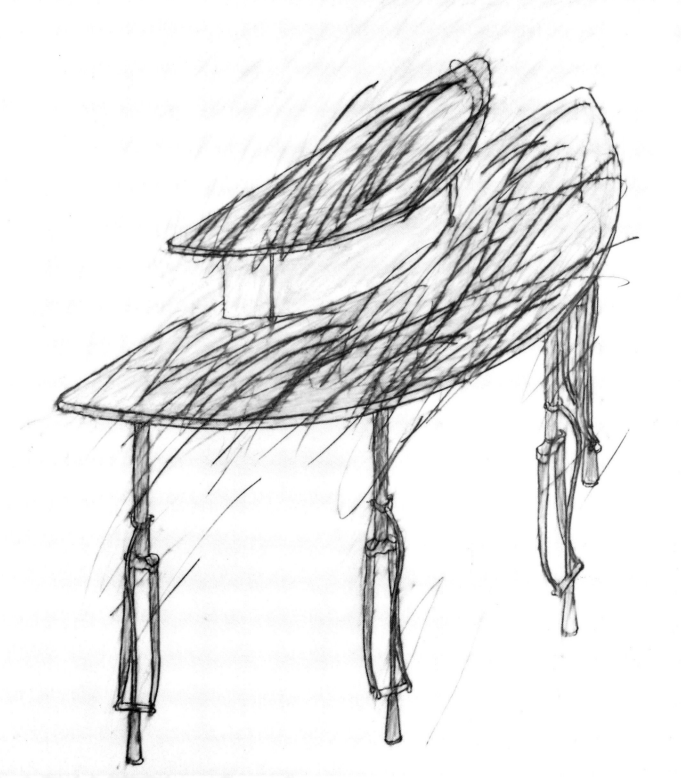

The Poetry of the Machine

Hugh Aldersey-Williams

A Blueprint Monograph

Published by
FOURTH ESTATE
AND WORDSEARCH,
LONDON

RIZZOLI
NEW YORK

First published in Great Britain in 1991 by Fourth Estate Ltd, 289 Westbourne Grove, London W11 2QA in conjunction with Blueprint Magazine, 26 Cramer Street, London W1M 3HE

A catalogue record for this book is available from the British Library

ISBN 1-872180-42-6

Design Alan Aboud
Series editors Vicky Wilson and Arthur Valenzuela
Colour reproduction Imago Publishing
Printed and bound in Italy

First published in the United States of America in 1991 by Rizzoli International Publications, Inc., 300 Park Avenue South, New York 10010

LC 90-50821
ISBN 0-8478-1358-4

Photographic credits

Satoshi Bando 88, 105, 106, 107, 110/11; Alessandro Gui 75; Alastair Hunter 13, 92; Impuls 71, 72, 73; Eliot Kausman 79; Tommaso Pellegrini 29, 30, 32, 50, 54, 55, 56, 57, 69, 77, 78, 80; Phil Sayer front cover; Andrea Zani 26, 31, 32, 36, 37, 38, 40, 41, 44, 45, 46, 47, 48, 49, 51, 62, 63, 67, 68, 70, 86, 87, 90, 91, 94, 95, 97, 98/9, 100, 101, 103, back cover.

The publishers would like to thank Interdecor Inc. of Japan for their assistance in the preparation of this monograph.

Acknowledgments
I should like to thank the following for their time and insight:
Sergio Gandini, Stephen Kiviat, Annibale Mandelli, Marco Pezzolo, Piero Portoghese, Yann Thomas, Pilar Viladas, Robert Webster and Renzo Zorzi. Delia Pertici Fraschini was an invaluable interpreter. Daniela and the staff at Studio King-Miranda suffered my intrusion with great fortitude and kindness. Finally, thanks to Perry and Santiago for a week of memorable conversations and memorable lunches. *Hugh Aldersey-Williams*

Blueprint Monographs
Ron Arad Restless Furniture
Deyan Sudjic
Nigel Coates The City in Motion
Rick Poynor
Rei Kawakubo and Comme des Garçons
Deyan Sudjic
Eva Jiricna Design in Exile
Martin Pawley

Contents

There is one question about the work of the Englishman Perry King and the Spaniard Santiago Miranda to which everybody wants the answer. It is simply this: who does what?

Several things encourage enquiry. First is the scrupulously equal front the two designers present. All their projects carry both their names. The one is most reluctant to be briefed by a client or interviewed by a journalist without the presence of the other. An apparently equal duo of designers is rare anywhere, but especially so in Milan, where it is the custom for a largely anonymous studio to produce work bearing the signature of one master. Second is the intriguing combination of these particular nationalities. If you were to select two European national stereotypes, you could hardly pick ones more different than the supposedly sensible, reserved English and the supposedly fiery, emotional Spanish.

Then there is the range, broad even by Milan's polymath standards, of design projects that the studio has undertaken over the years. King and Miranda began working together in 1972, designing typefaces for use on computer screens for Olivetti. This led into general graphics and the design of machine interfaces for the same company. In 1975, King and Miranda formally entered into partnership. They began work on a series of lamps for

Flos /Arteluce and on office furniture for Marcatré, the Milan-based firm. They have completed designs for the interiors of all Marcatré's showrooms around Europe, and this in turn has opened up opportunities for other interior design and small-scale architectural projects, notably in Japan. More recently, they have extended their exploration of furniture design, developing relations with a number of adventurous Spanish

King and Miranda's first project for Olivetti in 1972 was to devise an alphabet for computer print-outs. Their proposal was adopted by the European Computer Manufacturers' Association

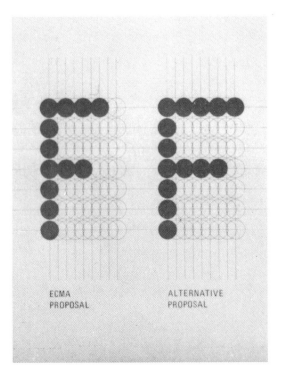

ECMA
PROPOSAL

ALTERNATIVE
PROPOSAL

manufacturers. In 1989, King and Miranda crowned their success in Spain by winning the commission to design the external lighting for the International Expo that will be held in 1992 in Seville, Miranda's home-town.

There is a final reason for wanting to know who does what. And that is that we are not meant to know. Ever polite – truly one of their shared qualities, with old-fashioned English gentlemanliness meeting Spanish *hidalgo* half-way – King and Miranda gently steer conversation away from any investigation of their individual creative characters. This is partly a mechanism to protect against unwarranted prying into the nature of their creativity, but one suspects it also amuses them to be evasive while people persist in trying to separate and analyse what should not be separated and analysed.

King and Miranda's sophistry is forgivable. Interlopers in the Italian design scene, they have had to create a myth about themselves to catch up with, and yet remain distinct from, the greats of Milanese design, who come with their own myths ready built. Today, Ettore Sottsass and Alessandro Mendini may have largely passed the *maestro* mantle on to Mario Bellini and Michele de Lucchi, but the society of Italian design remains a fairly closed one. Fortified by exclusive relationships with

prestigious manufacturers and editorships of influential journals, these men are no mere designers. They call themselves *architetti*, as do most who are schooled in Italy.

King and Miranda are not trained as architects. This makes them outsiders in Milanese terms, but it also goes some way towards making their design what it is. They point out that some of the most influential figures in Italian design in past decades, designers such as Joe Colombo and Carlo Mollino, were not primarily architects by training. And their clients seem to welcome the change. Sergio Gandini, the president of Flos, says: "They express the culture of their times. For a start, they are not the fourth generation of architects in the same family. Coming from a different tradition, they are designers first and foremost. Their starting point is pragmatic problem solving, which is not to say that they ignore the cultural dimension of design and all that goes with it."

King and Miranda have no manifesto and no political agenda. If they effect change, then it is through their work. That they are not architects means they do not, as some *architetti* can, approach what is specifically a design problem as a chore, filling in time before the next architectural commission comes along. Where the *architetto* might favour the grand

Above: The Palio table lamp, designed in 1984 for Arteluce, derives its name from the saddleback shape of its polished aluminium or copper reflector – rich materials that give an industrial lamp craft resonances
Right: The expressive cantilever of the back legs of the Esperona chair, 1988, suggests an air of suspended animation

plan, King and Miranda are willing and able to go into the finest detail, as at the beginning of their joint career, when they were designing typefaces for Olivetti. Yet though they may be debarred from calling themselves architects, King and Miranda do not complain when it happens by accident, as in an interview in a French magazine at the time of the inauguration of their Paris showroom for Marcatré, at a point when to work on larger,

more architectural projects was becoming a logical ambition.[1]

In private, though, the designers could perhaps afford to let down their guard. Do their two homes reveal their true sensibilities? Writer Anna Terzi finds in Miranda's 1984 flat that: "The careful choice of soft colours, even the two old armchairs of German design, lead back to a northern way of living."[2] King's more recent apartment, shown anonymously in *Abitare*,[3] is the product of the firm's wish to create a domestic interior for its portfolio. As such, it perhaps has rather more King and Miranda design, including some rejects and prototypes, than King would like. He would prefer a more monastic style, with bare bulbs in place of the Jill lamps that haunt his life. But overall, with its Driade kitchen and furniture from Cassina, it shows a willing adoption of Italian design.

So King and Miranda have little difficulty in making the transition into each other's cultural territory (interestingly, their wives Daniela and Elisabeth are respectively Italian and German; their common language is Italian). But perhaps as important in their shared experience is the fact that both have fled less than satisfactory surroundings in their native lands for the stimulation of Milan. Born in 1947, Santiago Miranda left Spain in 1971,

The enigmatically named Bloom bookshelf, 1988, is one of a series of sheet-metal products for the Italian firm T70

while General Francisco Franco was still in power. Before emigrating, he attended the backward-looking Escuela de Artes Aplicadas y Oficios Artísticos in Seville. At that time, the late 1960s, there was a move at the school to introduce a more realistic industrial emphasis by bringing in manufacturers from Barcelona and Bilbão. But the attempt was half-hearted and the school's curriculum remained rooted in the applied arts. "It was craftsmanship they were interested in. It didn't matter whether it was old or modern. The school had no

opinion on the contemporary." So Miranda dabbled in drawing, composition, model-making, pottery and sculpture before specialising in industrial design – a discipline regarded with deep suspicion by the Franco régime – for his final three years.

The Seville education was not entirely unproductive, however. Miranda acquired an unusual sensitivity to the traditions of local culture, which led him to seek out equivalent subtleties in the contemporary. "I am very interested in the tradition of my environment in Seville, in this very baroque Spanish situation. I became convinced that the modern world was just as baroque as the old one; it was just that the symbols weren't as evident." This ability to uncover symbols in the apparently banal has become a hallmark of King and Miranda's work, whether in the design of electronic equipment control panels or the creation of theatrical showrooms.

Nine years Miranda's senior, Perry King studied industrial design at the Birmingham College of Art. He won a scholarship for a final year's study, to be taken either before or after National Service. He chose to defer the postgraduate year, thinking it would be more rewarding if he came to it with greater maturity. As it happened, National Service was abolished while King was halfway through, a waste of two years that still rankles.

Nevertheless, that final year proved critical. King's teacher was Naum Slutzky from the Bauhaus, whose presence served to sharpen the counterpoint between orthodox modernism and the alternatives that were just beginning to emerge. Bauhaus philosophy was still highly influential in the mid-1950s; its successor schools at Ulm and in Chicago were flourishing and there was a diaspora of former Bauhaus teachers spreading the gospel around the world. But against this backdrop of functionalism, a subversive bombshell was to drop. It was in the Italian magazine, *Stile Industria*, that King first saw the Elea 9003 computer, designed for Olivetti by Ettore Sottsass. This was pure enough in form; it presented crisp square and rectangular elevations that would please any functionalist. But its richness of materials distinguished it from similar designs. Its door was a solid slab of aluminium, perhaps a centimetre thick, not the flimsy, pressed sheet that the same machine would have had if it had been made in Britain at that time. King's notion of what design could be – and what it was likely never to be in Britain – was changed forever.

This was at the end of the 1950s. It may be facetious to compare the comparative cultural and material poverty of Britain in the 1950s with that of Spain a decade later, but it remains that when King and Miranda left their respective shores they were seeking departure and escape as much as arrival somewhere new.

1. "Architecture et Politique d'Image, Les Show-rooms de Marcatré", *Architecture Intérieure Crée*, April/May 1989.
2. A. Terzi, "Santiago Miranda", *Interni*, September 1984, pp.18-19.
3. "Ogni Anno una Parete Nuova", *Abitare*, November 1989, pp.134-9.

Murals for the London
Marcatré showroom,
1985-86, depict in
a romanticised way
the transmission of
information from hand
to page, mouth to
ear and page to eye
involved in writing,
talking and reading

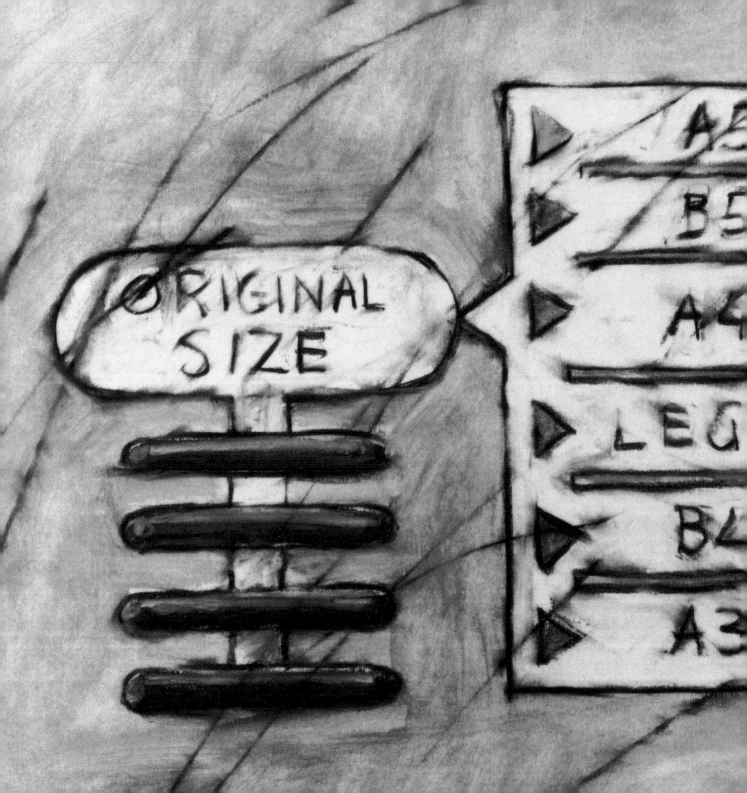

After some years working in the genteel obscurity of a British design consultancy, Perry King arrived in Milan in 1965 and succeeded in gaining a place in the studio where the Elea 9003 had been conceived. One of the projects to which King was assigned was to become a still better-known object within the Sottsass output. A new portable typewriter for Olivetti, it was in one sense very much a product of its time – a bright red, fun-loving, flower-power alternative to the heavy grey office machine, and with a friendly name to boot. "It is called Valentine and was invented for use any place except in an office, so as not to remind anyone of monotonous working hours, but rather to keep amateur poets company on quiet Sunday afternoons in the country..."[1]

For the type of product it was, the Valentine was undeniably ahead of its time. It was no mean feat in those days for Sottsass and King to have created a typewriter that so clearly signalled through its form, colour and detailing the wish not to be associated with typewriters that had gone before, even including Marcello Nizzoli's Lettera 22, on which the design was partly based. But the image the Valentine acquired through advertising was equally important to its success. Sottsass personally was very involved

in this, something new and of interest to King: "This was a big experience for me, an insight into what I thought then and consider now to be a correct approach." The image of the Valentine that persists today was created through posters by the American graphic designer Milton Glaser, who reproduced settings from classical paintings, substituting the little red typewriter for a human figure or other detail. The technique as well as the approach must have made a great impact on King, for twenty years later it is still how King and Miranda have chosen sometimes to illustrate their own work. The technique is used particularly effectively in "Lonely Tools", an exhibition of their work that toured Europe during 1990.

After five years with Sottsass, King left the studio and went travelling with his wife, Daniela. The year-long journey took them to India and Japan, among other places. King was very ill upon his return and required a number of major operations. The illness transformed his sense of urgency and purpose in life. "From being somebody who was always waiting for it to happen, I thought I'd better start to make it happen." King recalled the man who had moved into his house in Britain when he had come to Milan, a composer who filled the bookshelves with symphonies he had written

King and Miranda's design for the exhibition catalogue *Design Process: Olivetti 1908-1979*. The spread shows Milton Glaser's posters for Olivetti products, including the Sottsass-designed Valentine typewriter

but never heard. King resolved that it was not going to be like that for him.

Recuperating slowly from his illness, King was not a particularly attractive employment prospect. So he was fortunate when Renzo Zorzi at Olivetti offered him a job for which it would seem he was uniquely unqualified: that of design co-ordinator with special responsibility for typeface design. Now an independent consultant to Olivetti, Zorzi had come to know King while the designer was working with Sottsass. Zorzi's responsibilities at Olivetti were wide-ranging, covering corporate identity and advertising as well as product design. It is typically Anglo-Saxon to worry that one person should have responsibility for all these disciplines, just as it is typically Anglo-Saxon to worry about

King's supposed lack of qualifications for the job Zorzi was offering.

Such bureaucratic literal-mindedness has little place in Italian culture. Like IBM, which took its lead from the Italian company, Olivetti has a corporate image expressed through its architecture and products as well as its graphics and advertising. But Olivetti, especially when it was still owned by the Olivetti family, was more liberal, its employees more able to choose whether to conform or not. Zorzi was more impressed by King's willingness to get to grips with a substantial problem than worried about his lack of formal qualifications in graphic design or typography. King makes no pretence about his own inexperience. The only point in his favour, he quips now, is that his father knew Eric Gill.

It was in 1971, shortly after this job commenced, that Perry King and Santiago Miranda met at a party. The subject of their first conversation was food, something that has remained of inordinate importance in their lives ever since. King had completed work on a corporate identity manual inherited in a half-finished state from Clino Castelli and Hans von Klier, Olivetti's director of corporate identity under Zorzi, and moved on to tackle the design of typefaces for use on computer screens. It soon became apparent that the project was virtually limitless. Each character had to be designed and evaluated for readability (the ease with which it could be identified in isolation) and legibility (the ease with which it could be identified in the context of other characters or words). King recommended that Miranda be brought in to assist and Zorzi agreed. "Zorzi recognised in us a desire and a capability to look into projects which other designers perhaps did not have the time or inclination or curiosity to look at," says Miranda.

Even among designers, typography is an arcane field. One of its handful of experts was Arturo Rolfo at Olivetti. He successfully and, given his expertise, perhaps justifiably blocked any innovation the two upstarts wished to make. But at least they were in the best company: Herbert Lindinger, Wim Crouwel and Joseph Müller-Brockmann had all been commissioned by Olivetti at one time or another, and none of their designs pursued.

King and Miranda's strength was to see that the brief could not be met solely by considerations of design and typography. The typefaces that Olivetti required were to be machine-readable and had to improve on a proposal from the European Computer Manufacturers' Association about which Olivetti was unhappy. The designers went to Olivetti's head of research to ask him to appoint an engineer to collaborate with them on the technological aspect of the design. The job of the engineer, Alberto Brunetti, was to refine the proposed design for each alphanumeric symbol, correcting for the impact of the 7×9 dot-matrix printer on the paper so that the letters would appear as continuous as possible.

At the conclusion of their research, King and Miranda put together a highly polished presentation of their findings. The combination of the thoroughness of the study and the slickness with which it was presented impressed the ECMA engineers, and the modified proposals were accepted. King and Miranda outlined the principles they had adopted as follows: "The guiding criterion used in the evaluation and in the design of the alternative proposals to ensure maximum legibility and human acceptance has been to imbue the figures with a high degree of what [the ergonomist] R. S. Easterby calls 'figural goodness'.... Those qualities contributing to 'figural goodness' include simplicity, unity and lack of superimposed forms. In particular it was felt that the shape of each letter should be as near as possible to that in common use.... That the continuity of line in a symbol is more important than the density of points in that line. That closed spaces should be kept as large as possible and that the symmetric or asymmetric quality of a symbol should be emphasised as far as is compatible with the design of a font with an organic unity of form and weight." [2]

Riding on this success, King and Miranda gained Olivetti's trust and were able to go ahead with additional font design projects, not only for optical character recognition but for use on visual display terminals. In addition to testing each proposed character design for legibility at three different resolutions (7 vertical dots by 5 horizontally, 7×7 and 7×9), King and Miranda now had to test each version twice, once for its suitability for display white-on-black on a luminous computer screen, and once black-on-white for printed documents. On top of all this was the now familiar but ever gruelling 100 kilometre commute between Milan and Olivetti's headquarters in Ivrea, near Turin.

Once again, King and Miranda's response to the problem was iconoclastic. For the 7×7 font, they invented a double baseline, different for upper- and lower-case letters, as a way of retaining satisfactory legibility for individual characters while still fitting capitals, lower-case with ascenders and lower-case with descenders within the constraining 7×7 matrix. As in the work on interface design that they were later to do for Olivetti, ergonomic conventional wisdom would have deemed the solution unacceptable. And though the designers too knew their proposal was inherently wrong, they recognised it as less wrong than the alternatives available with the low-resolution technology.

As often happens, King and Miranda's reading of the ergonomic literature had suggested no satisfactory approach. The brief was to solve a problem raised by the advent of a new technology, whereas published ergonomic data and guidance are necessarily based on the analysis of user-tests with equipment that already exists. The only option was to take a leap in the dark and follow up with their own assessments. Fortunately the

mr leopold bloom ate w
of beasts and fowls h
nutty gizzards a stuff
fried with crustcrumbs
of all he liked grille
to his palate a fine t
kidneys were in his mi
kitken softly rightin

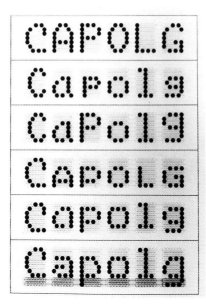

King and Miranda's typographic design project for Olivetti of 1973 included designs for fonts for a 7x5, 7x7 and 7x9 dot matrix. The problems to be solved included the incorporation of the accents required in various languages, far left, and the display of lower-case script within the 7-dot vertical range, left. In the latter case, the ascenders and descenders were accommodated by using a double-baseline scheme, above

designers' position at Olivetti had by now
become sufficiently powerful that the
company's ergonomists could not veto the
proposals before they had been tried. It was
a victory for empiricism over dogmatism.

Within the international community of
designers, and especially among the superstars
of Milan, Paris and Barcelona, ergonomics
is not much discussed. Its importance is
underplayed by designers as well as by the
design press and a designer who places
ergonomics high on his or her list of priorities
is often perceived as over-earnest or plodding.
Ergonomists too do themselves few favours by
scorning designers generally and perpetuating
a split between the practice of ergonomics as
a science and the utilisation of ergonomics in
design. Despite their unwillingness to follow
the injunctions of ergonomists too literally,
King and Miranda have shown in the body of
their work that sound ergonomic sense and
uncompromisingly individual design can go
hand in hand. Though they play it down to the
media, these rigorous beginnings are no small
ingredient in what makes the design of King
and Miranda special, both in the broad context
of international repute and in the local context
of Milanese creativity.

King and Miranda and their work were
liked by Olivetti, but the duo did not feel
especially secure in their relationship with
their client. During the period they were
working on the typefaces, they began a project
of their own, which they called Unlimited
Horizon. These were hard times. All the
Olivetti earnings (not as much as might be
thought, they insist) were swallowed up by this
extra-curricular study. Apart from anything
else, Unlimited Horizon was a form of
experiential research to determine whether
and how King and Miranda would work
together. They proved their creative
relationship by surviving this difficult period
and remain proud that they did so without
compromising their design by taking work
solely for commercial reasons. Ideas first
expressed in the Unlimited Horizon project,
a year's worth of drawings dating from 1975
and 1976, have since appeared in much of
King and Miranda's produced design,
especially in furniture.

Towards the end of 1975, more than
three years after they had first met, King and
Miranda formally entered into partnership.
Though known as King-Miranda Associati,
the glass door to their studio, newly located in
a former cement works behind Milan's Porta
Genova station near the *navigli*, retains the
legend "Unlimited Horizon SRL". (The title
is a pun, since the initials are the Italian

abbreviation for a *limited* company.) In the context of its Italian surroundings, the firm, with the typically English and Spanish names of its principals, still sounds slightly exotic.

The studio itself seems designed to sustain a certain myth regarding the principals' creative process. In the middle of the space, sandwiched between the open studio on one side and the reception and conference areas on the other, is an inner sanctum. It is here, behind closed doors, that King and Miranda generate their ideas. There are no fixed roles. There is no straight-man, funny-man routine. The privacy allows apparently crazy ideas to be mooted by either party without risk of ridicule. Working at a square table, they typically will start drawing together, sketching, re-sketching and laying over sheets of tracing paper to refine the form of a design. The designers from the studio participate in the next stage, realising the sketch in three dimensions. They are left to get on with the work, the idea being to encourage them to identify with the project through intimate association. They are given very little creative freedom, however, and choose to work there because they wish to learn. It is an apprenticeship typical of many Milan studios.

King and Miranda do argue, though in client meetings they more commonly present a united front. The effect is to give clients the impression it all comes easily. "I never wondered where they get their ideas from," says Piero Portoghese. "It seems so natural. In Italian we say of an artist that his work is *felice*…some designers may endlessly work and rework their ideas, but I never think of Santiago and Perry agonising over a problem through the night," he adds. Appearances can be deceptive, but King and Miranda are certainly not about to alter this perception.

Although it is impossible to separate the ingredients of King and Miranda's creative personality, it is clear that it is King who is the more serious when it comes to running the business. It is he who cracks the whip; it is his wife, Daniela, who is in charge of administration. It was he who grew apoplectic when he discovered, while helping to gather photographs for this book, that everything was not quite where it ought to be in the studio's extensive archive. Santiago cannot take such matters seriously and seeks to diffuse the tension with a light-hearted remark or a change of subject. By Milan standards, they run a tight ship indeed.

King and Miranda's grounding in the dry disciplines of corporate identity and typography presented a far from complete picture of their interests and abilities, a problem they solved on a personal level by the unpublicised Unlimited Horizon work. But before long the Olivetti graphics programme was providing opportunities for more personal projects. King and Miranda's first poster for the company presented its typefaces through a colourful, frivolous design that was very much an antidote to the typefaces themselves.

The work that followed – the posters "Olivetti in the World" and "Grande Quadrato Magico" and the book *Design Process* – shared many of the same characteristics. These designs were often diagrammatic to the point of being narrative. King and Miranda have always seen their graphics as a means of connection; their approach to the discipline is ideas-based rather than aesthetically based and they are always happier when their designs are built around one of their own projects. The Olivetti posters were enriched with a rainbow of bold colours and hand-drawn background textures. The designs had depth, often recalling the naïve perspectives of the Early Renaissance or the exaggerated perspectives of Surrealism. The eclectic imagery and typography, the mix of colours and other recurring themes, such as the graded backgrounds that fade like a Mediterranean sky from dark blue at the top to pale blue at the bottom, distinguish these posters as

typically Latin. Certainly, this is not graphic design of the Swiss school.

In the overall context of the Olivetti image, King and Miranda's graphics stand out. In common with most large companies during the 1960s and 1970s, Olivetti had generally adopted Swiss-style graphic design. Franco Bassi's advertisements and layouts for annual reports were described as "the expression of a pure graphic fantasy, where color and sign are fused in a compelling unity supporting a concise printed communication",[3] although the compositions are pure Swiss. Walter Ballmer, who designed the present version of the Olivetti logotype as well as advertising graphics, was trained in Switzerland.

A pertinent observation about the connection between the design of products and graphics by King and Miranda comes from Renzo Zorzi. During the early 1980s, King and Miranda designed the 2510 photocopier and, with Antonio Macchi-Cassia, the M10 personal computer for Olivetti as well as a number of products for Black and Decker and McCulloch Italia.

"They have given a new look to Olivetti products," Zorzi wrote, "perhaps because they were developed in a particularly important moment, during a break (led by post-modernism and, in Italy, by Memphis) with

Above: In the "Grande Quadrato Magico" poster for Olivetti, 1980, a magic square (each horizontal, vertical and corner-to-corner diagonal line adds up to 131,104) hovers in a landscape that recalls Giorgio de Chirico or Max Ernst

Right: King and Miranda's posters are often characterised by a stage-like composition with planar areas of colour and texture and a graded sky

OLIVETTI   IN   THE   WORLD

With its use of colour, perspective and texture, this 1976 Olivetti poster has little in common with the Swiss purism prevalent in graphic design of the time

careful arrangement on a page, the balance of their densities."[4]

Alongside graphics commissions for Olivetti, King and Miranda began to take on other graphics work, to the point where it looked as if this was where their future might lie. One particularly promising job was the design of a corporate identity for the Spanish company, Norma Europa. It would have been King and Miranda's first job outside Italy, but the company went bankrupt, owing a substantial amount in fees. One can only speculate about the direction King and Miranda's career might have taken had Norma Europa survived. As it was, their attention turned to other aspects of design, although they have continued to produce graphics to promote their own Marcatré chairs and Arteluce lamps. A poster for the Air Mail chairs was particularly engaging, using the motifs and crinkly, thin paper of air mail letters.

The "new look to Olivetti products" that Zorzi attributes to King and Miranda gained much of its impetus from the feel for visual images and figurative representation that they brought to bear on their graphics. And from 1982, that thinking was applied instead to the design of the interfaces – the keyboards and instrument panels – of Olivetti machines.

formal conventions. In terms of architecture and product design (where I think the movement barely touched on the borders of existing manufacturing) there is plenty left to say about the possibility of further progress.… Graphic design, and with it the use of new colour tones and contrasts, is a different case. This field seems to be carving out something new and strong in visual images as well as in figurative representation, moving away from a fairly frigid form of graphic symmetry in which expression became little more than an exaltation of the typographic characters, their

Opposite: The complexity achieved by the overlap of text and pictorial images in Assyrian relief work became the basis for some of King and Miranda's interface design projects
Below: The bold use of colour and formal values of the 1981 chain-saw for McCulloch Italia reveal King and Miranda's adaptation to Italian thinking in industrial design

Once again, King and Miranda exploited historical allusions to give the user a sense, purposely vague, of identification with the product. Miranda was able to put to good use an interest in Egyptology. He had noted that Egyptian writing places alphabetic characters alongside pictorial hieroglyphs and that for emphasis, glyphs are doubled by placing them back-to-back to create symmetrical new motifs that stand out from the surrounding script. Miranda thought these redundancies could be adapted to modern needs. "We work in the contemporary, but with the feeling that people of all cultures in the past have had the same anxieties about their situation. When Perry and I started with the Olivetti interface, we decided to consider the interfaces of all cultures like ours. This opened the door to archetypal symbols. I don't know why I am interested in these things, but I think it is based on the knowledge that people have been facing these problems all through mankind's history. We have had a conscious and an *unconscious* desire to research into and to use archetypal signs all through our work."

The exact meaning of the symbols to former cultures is unimportant; the new symbols are in any case abstract variations with no meaning outside their contemporary context. What is important is that the symbols should look as though they mean something; they should create an instinctive bridge rather than a conscious recognition. Once again, King and Miranda were perpetrating an ergonomic solecism for the greater good of the user. On a practical level, the redundancy of the symbols is of value since the user's view of a key is blocked while depressing it – an unnerving experience, especially for someone learning to use the equipment. Hence each symbol comprises two parts – one that is pressed and is hidden while pressed, with one that remains visible adjoining it.

The resulting symbols were grouped on each panel according to need, though the grouping was dictated to some extent by the use of the same parts for panels with different levels of function. This logic led to what Miranda calls "islands of information"

Right: Between 1982 and 1987 controls for Olivetti equipment developed from conventional pressed keys, top, via touch-sensitive relief keys to flush-mounted touch-sensitive keys given the appearance of texture, bottom

Below: A crucial step was the separation of the button from its function indication, as in this printer control panel

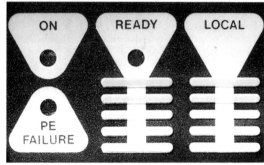

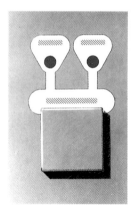

Above: Several keys employ symmetrical designs inspired by the ancient Egyptian habit of doubling hieroglyphs

Right: The granite-like
pattern used for the
flush-mounted touch-
sensitive keys, takes
further the reference
to writings on stone.
High technology is both
civilised and celebrated
by the historical
resonances

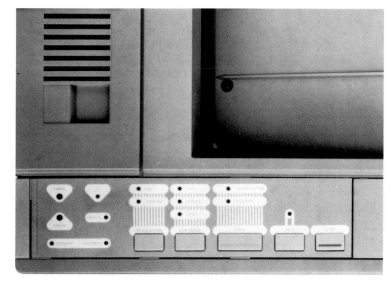

Left: The first
application of control
button designs based
on ideas from ancient
written communication
was on a facsimile
machine

A series of modular
plastic components
is used to identify
computer equipment
with similar casings but
different specifications

A series of modular
plastic components
is used to identify
computer equipment
with similar casings but
different specifications

scattered unevenly around an instrument panel. As a result the overall layout was often not very orderly. (This was frequently exacerbated by the fact that the graphics were to be overlaid on old panels rather than designed integrally with them. In other instances, Olivetti was buying made-up panels from Japan and asking King and Miranda for little more than a new colour scheme. The designers protested, reminding Olivetti that such expedience was out of line with the company's history of cultural patronage.) The King-Miranda designs earned some criticism for their difference, not least from Olivetti

engineers who resisted the innovation and, ironically, were coming up with their own neat, designerly layouts.

The designers had realised something about the machines that the engineers had not. "It was a case of reassessing the way people assumed you use a machine and its keyboard. Olivetti has an extremely wide knowledge of the ergonomics of the *professional* keyboard. Our contribution was to say: 'This isn't a professional keyboard, and all the parameters by which you are judging it are wrong. It's not what you think it is.'" And nor was it. This was equipment to be used in many cases by amateur keyboarders, a distinction that will become increasingly important in the future. Most designers currently consider interface design of this level of sophistication as something that matters only in office equipment. Through their Unlimited Horizon speculation and Olivetti studies, King and Miranda are among the leaders in designing for its potential importance in the home. None the less, the world of the office will continue to fuel developments in interface design. After defence, it is perhaps the area most likely to demand and best able to afford expensive new technologies.

Olivetti was conscious of the startling originality of King and Miranda's symbolic

The Olivetti M10 personal computer of 1983, below, designed with Antonio Macchi-Cassia, has a liquid-crystal display screen and was designed for portability

approach and some senior staff were worried that the market would not buy it. But the company held fast to its beliefs, not even carrying out any market research. Like Italian companies of all sizes, Olivetti is more inclined to trust its judgment than to subject every proposal to the sterilising scrutiny of public appraisal. With the combination of changing patterns of work in the office and the popularisation of post-modern architecture and graphic design, "Miranda was understanding better than anyone what it was all about," says Zorzi. "He understood what kinds of things could and should be changed given the new possibilities."

Miranda's knowledge of archaeology and ancient scripts was acquired out of interest, rather than specifically for this project. But in general, King and Miranda read widely and are assiduous in keeping up with trends in painting, architecture, film and other arts. The information and inspiration gleaned is stored for possible future use. And the flow often goes in the other direction, too: King and Miranda are always pleased to see a theme explored in their own work confirmed in other media. They believe that such exchange is crucial if designers are to be able to predict likely futures for our material environment. Among films, they cite Ridley Scott's *Bladerunner* and Michelangelo Antonioni's *Modesty Blaise* as intelligent scenarios that reveal possible aspects of sensory interaction between man and machine.

King and Miranda's designs evolved as keyboard technology advanced. What began as a three-dimensional key to be depressed manually soon became a touch-sensitive key with a slight relief so that it could be located by feel. The design was later modified to be completely flat to the touch, but with textural or *trompe l'œil* three-dimensional patterns. If anything, key function now had to be indicated more clearly because there was less movement involved in selecting a function.

Right: The clean form of the Olivetti 2510 photocopier of 1982 owes a debt to the Olivetti corporate image created before King and Miranda's involvement

Left: Studies for the Olivetti Experimental Personal Office Computer project, 1986-87, anticipated future developments in software

The design was to perform two roles which are largely contradictory: to respond to the marketing need to signify the presence of new technology while at the same time psychologically to calm and prepare the user for the change. This ability at once to express and to humanise new technology has become something of a King and Miranda art, seen not only in electronic equipment but also to a lesser extent in their lighting and furniture.

The only industrial design projects to take these ideas a stage further remain on the drawing-board. In 1986, King and Miranda embarked on the Experimental Personal Office Computer project under the aegis of Herman Hauser, Olivetti's director of research. This was an attempt to give form to computer peripherals that might be manufactured using technology that would become available during the next five years. The success of the project is indicated by the fact that the foam models of the studies – a desk-top photocopier, a fax machine and a flat-panel display terminal – do indeed look contemporary in 1991. Sadly, the EPOC project came to an end when Hauser left to set up the Active Book Company in Cambridge, England.

Another study, commissioned by Sony in Japan, explores similar technology for domestic applications. The work remains confidential – King and Miranda will describe their proposal only as an interactive electronic entertainment device, a design based on their own product concept. The project, though incomplete, begins to fulfil King and Miranda's wish to become more involved with product innovation and conception. They talk of a telephone for the deaf, an interactive fax machine, a photocopier with texture for use by the blind – not out of altruism, but because they see ways of bringing the unrealised potential of electronics into contact with real but unfulfilled needs and uses.

1. *Abitare*, No. 77, quoted in *Design Process Olivetti: 1908-1983*, p.122.
2. "Alternative Proposals for the European Computer Manufacturers' Association Font for 7x9 Matrix Printers", Olivetti internal document (unpublished).
3. *Design Process Olivetti: 1908-1983*, *ibid*, p.110.
4. R. Zorzi, "Introductory Note", in G. Barbacetto, *Design Interface: How Man and Machine Communicate. Olivetti Design and Research by King and Miranda*, Arcadia Edizioni, Milan, 1987, p.8.

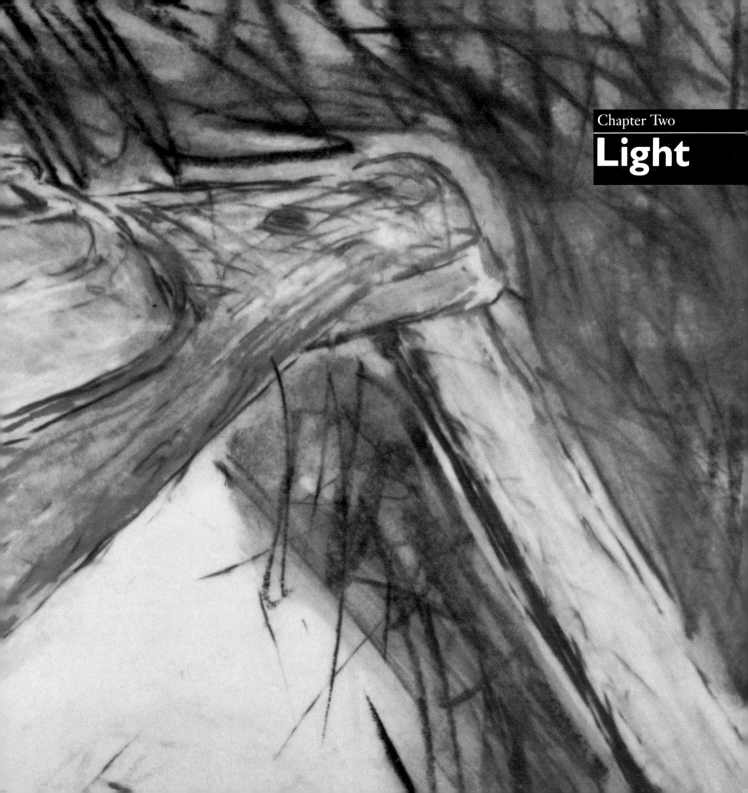

Below and opposite:
The Jill uplighter of
1977 showed that
high-tech halogen lamps
could be adapted to
domestic use

"I recently read of an experiment to measure the distance between the Earth and the moon," Perry King is quoted as saying in an article in *International Design.*[1] "The experiment itself I find curious, but the technology that was used is wonderfully poetic. The idea was to send a beam of light from the Earth to the moon and wait for its reflection to reach us. To receive moonlight not reflected from the Sun, but from our own light source – to have created moonlight – is a beautiful and dramatic thing!"

The interplay between technology and poetry informs much of King and Miranda's design. It is seen clearly in the interfaces for Olivetti products, but it is no less important in the lamps, a series of more than twenty designs produced over fifteen years for Flos/Arteluce. It is here that technology and poetry are fused most completely: "Perry and Santiago both support technological progress. They are fascinated by technology in an obvious way, but they haven't forgotten that science can be poetic too," notes the American design critic Pilar Viladas.

The word "forgotten" is well chosen. Especially in Anglo-Saxon Britain, Germany and the United States, the Greek meaning of the word technology, *techne* and *logos*, art and reason, seems to have been almost forgotten.

It is one of the attractions of Italy, and one of the reasons for its pre-eminence in design, that the connection between poetry and technology is forgotten less often than elsewhere. And it is this that drew King and Miranda and many others to practise in Milan.

King and Miranda's Jill light is not Flos president Sergio Gandini's favourite. But it is his bestseller. Jill became the quintessential uplighter and is King and Miranda's most popular and most successful design. Its structure – a simple steel tube joining a base and a light-diffusing dish – is as minimal as can be imagined. The material of both the diffuser and the base is frosted pressed glass, a robust yet elegant antidote to the blown glass commonly used in arts-and-crafts Italian lamps. This is exciting for two reasons: it resolves the composition – two glass forms are balanced at the ends of the black metal pole – and the glass clearly bears the weight of the lamp, something that would be impossible with conventional blown glass.

But Gandini prefers the El light. He and his vice-president, Marco Pezzolo, find it more innovative and technically better. El stands as tall as Jill, but appears more technocratic – a hard-edged constructivist collage of angled metal castings in red and black, in which the white light fixture forms a contrasting accent.

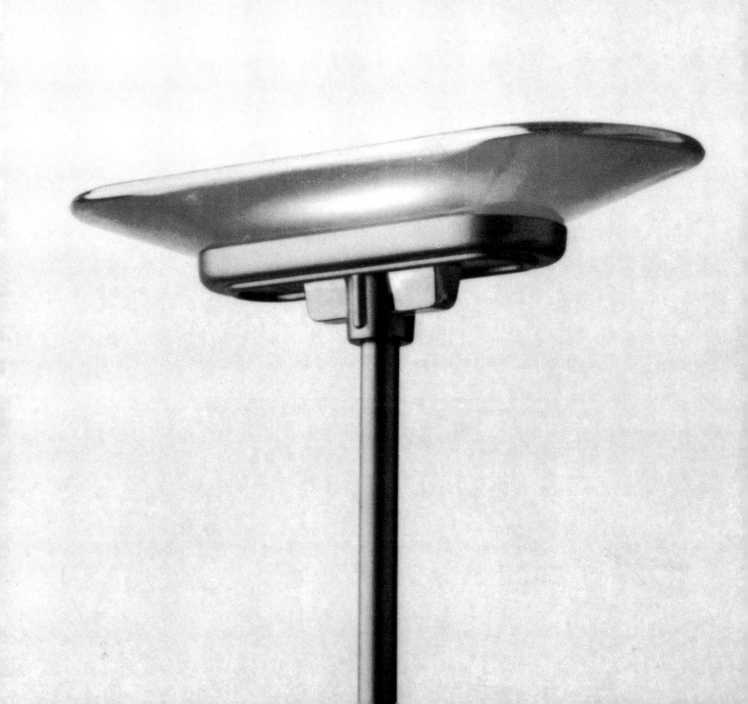

The less domestic
contemporary of the
Jill, the El lamp, 1978,
was much admired by
Arteluce staff but
remained in production
for only a short time

Jill and El were two of a series of six lamps presented to Flos in 1977. Flos had just acquired another lighting manufacturer, Arteluce, and needed a collection of lamps as an indication to the market of its wish to revise its policy of patronage under the new name. Flos had long promoted a closed collection of designs, with Achille Castiglioni and Tobia Scarpa its only appointed designers. Arteluce, meanwhile, had developed under the aegis of its designer-owner, Gino Sarfatti. As so often happens, the company found to its cost that a designer-owner could not both design and manage. But when Sarfatti retired, the way was opened for a change of direction. Flos wanted the company to become more responsive to the market, less dependent on one man's taste. It proposed an open collection, whereby Arteluce would be free to commission new designers as occasion arose, while Flos would retain its court designers.

In winning the commission to design the first lamps for the new Arteluce, King and Miranda got the break they badly needed and a chance to work with a high degree of creative freedom for a well-respected manufacturer. As fate would have it, the good news came through on the same day that the designers heard that their Spanish hope, Norma Europa, had collapsed. King and Miranda were not to set professional foot in Spain for another decade, while their stock began at last to rise in Italy.

The relationship between King and Miranda and Flos/Arteluce began as it has continued ever since, with a high level of generosity on both sides. King believes that one reason they were able to elbow their way into the august company of Castiglioni and Scarpa was the sheer overkill of their first, speculative presentation. King and Miranda showed six designs, light-heartedly christened Dolly, Donald, Mantis and Caterina, in addition to Jill and El. Each was presented in a comprehensive series of drawings sufficient not only to give the company's leadership a clear impression of how the lamps would appear if manufactured, but also to convince the company's engineers that the designers had given thought to the details of fabrication. The designs were developed in collaboration with Gianluigi Arnaldi, a former Olivetti engineer and an associate in the early days of the King-Miranda studio. Later, the designers learned to work closely with the client's own engineering staff.

The method King and Miranda had adopted in their painstaking work for Olivetti was to work here too. Such thoroughness has characterised their work – and, equally

Left: With its bright peaked cap, Donald is the most evocative of King and Miranda's 1977-78 lamps

Right: Dolly, and Caterina, far right, were among the range of six lamps King and Miranda proposed to Flos/Arteuce in 1977-78. It was to be the beginning of a long-term creative relationship

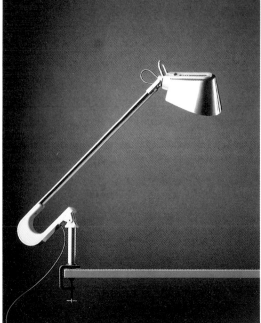

important, the presentation of that work to clients – ever since. The apparent completeness of a project in presentation serves not only to persuade clients of the designers' seriousness and of the feasibility of their designs, but also goes a long way towards forestalling unwanted meddling by company engineers or patrons who turn out to be frustrated designers themselves. If a project appears complete, and if the designers can defend every detail at an early stage, it is hard for a client to argue.

Flos/Arteluce put five of the King-Miranda lights into production. Two of them flopped, three were successful, and the Jill became a legend, the accessory without which no 1980s design studio or advertising agency was complete. Gandini, though impressed at the number and detail of King and Miranda's proposals, sensed that not all of them would find a ready market. However, he decided to fall in with his new designers' enthusiasm, thinking it would be salutary to show them the hard way that some of their designs were unlikely to be viable and being prepared to bear the cost of demonstrating this. This exercise in market education was important experience. Arteluce was now growing, increasing its investment, expanding production runs and taking greater risks.

Lamps were not usually produced in high volumes at this time, so the market would grow in line with Arteluce's ability both to educate and to satisfy its public.

King and Miranda, meanwhile, had educated Gandini, who was stunned at the popularity of the Jill. The achievement of the design was to use industrial materials and processes to create a lamp that was predominantly domestic in character. Italian shops are full of lamps that use traditional blown glass from Murano and elsewhere. King and Miranda have no objection to this sort of craft process (their vases and bowls for Veart show them willing to work in this idiom when it suits them). But in the case of the Jill, they wanted to make a lamp with entirely new qualities. They were not interested in the thinness and surface quality of hand-crafted glass, but in the ability of manufactured glass to diffuse light in an interesting way.

Halogen illumination was just beginning to enter the home at this time, and for reasons of their expense and novel appearance, such lamps were considered "high tech". King and Miranda wished to hide the bulb, while still making the best use of its high brightness. They had decided that pressed glass would produce the right overall lighting effect, but had not realised how large the production runs needed to be in order for this process to be viable. Pressed glass had an industrial heritage and an industrial appearance, yet it was not a new material – it had been used before in Flos designs by Castiglioni. "We should not exaggerate the technology," says Gandini. "We were not going to the moon."

What was new in King and Miranda's Jill lamp was the transfer of this material to the domestic setting, and here colour became an important factor. Aware that the scale of production would make frequent changes of glass colour an impossibility, King and Miranda investigated bottle plants and other industrial works where glass parts were manufactured. A key moment in the creative process was to think what colours are made in

large runs for other applications, hence the cobalt blue of pharmaceutical glass and the amber of traffic-light diffusers became the two initial colours of the Jill lamp in addition to white. In combination with a light source of up to 500 watts, the colours gained a new vibrancy in their unaccustomed interior settings. Grey and rose glass diffusers joined the range later and a bracket-held version called Wall followed in 1978.

There is a certain perversity in the designers' use of an industrial material to effect the transition of the new technology of halogen lamps from the commercial environment to the domestic arena. That King and Miranda did this by adding technology of their own to express the technological content of the lamps, rather than by disguising it with traditional craft and decorative devices, is a tribute to their ability as designers. In effect, they deliberately made the problem more difficult before solving it. Yet in the end, this solution is less to do with the "high-tech" pressed glass than with the skilful hiding of the real technology of the lamp. Its bulb is usually invisible, hidden from the normal level of gaze below the horizon of the glass diffuser; wires and switches are as discreet as possible; the lamp has a friendly personality in its name. As in the interface design for Olivetti, new

technology has been flagged and humanised in the same design.

"Jill was designed at a time when all halogen lamps were little machines," says King. "What attracted us to the halogen bulb was the intense white quality of its light, obtained with a relatively low wattage. We were interested in designing a light which was going to be in contract and domestic use. Because of the work we had been doing on Unlimited Horizon, we were also convinced that many of the differences between contract and domestic were artificial, having arisen either as a result of economic pressures or because of dimensional differences between the spaces, which were tending to disappear.

"It was, of course, a priority for us to get away from this machine aesthetic of the object. Our concern was to provide a surrounding that was an expression of people's perception of the light, rather than of their perception of the technology."

It is perhaps surprising that less appears to have been written about King and Miranda's lamps than about other aspects of their work. Individually, many of them are among the designers' strongest pieces; they are the works that are least interfered with during design development. And as a series, they are the clearest indicator of the designers' concerns

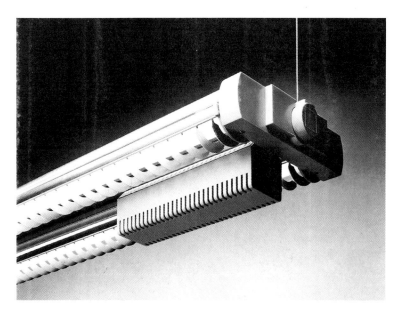

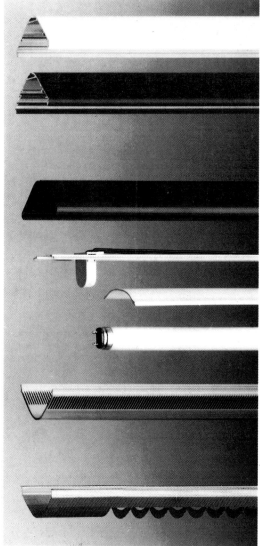

Above and right: In their most conventional configuration, the fluorescent tubes of the Expanded Line system may be arranged each side of the central wiring channel or a single tube hung below it. Wiring channels can be plugged together rather than fixed by screws

Opposite and far right: The Halley lighting system of 1979 aimed to bring elegance to office lighting by removing the power source from the lighting fixture

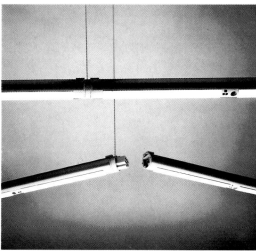

Above: Ra is one of several lamps designed to be used with the Expanded Line system
Opposite: With the Aurora, 1982, King and Miranda tamed the harsh halogen-lamp technology with a design based on a sandwich of mass-manufactured glass and methacrylate discs

and influences and of their evolution over a decade and a half in practice together. Yet this is not to say that one design will always be a linear development from its antecedents. Alongside the seraphic Jill, for example, Donald, Monkey and Mantis are effective zoomorphic jokes. And contemporary with these projects is the very different Halley, a lighting system intended for the office rather than the home.

Halley was an attempt to bring a degree of elegance to commercial fluorescent lighting, achieved by removing the power source from the lighting fixture, which could then hang freely and appear more lightweight. In the case of the Halley, the diamond-shaped section of the hanging fixtures is a functional way of containing the tube, reflector, wiring duct and moulded methacrylate or metal gauze diffuser within a minimum elegant geometry.

Halley was in many ways the dress rehearsal for Expanded Line, a still more minimal integrated system of slung lighting in which fluorescent tubes are held by their ends as free-hanging rods of light, recalling the light sculptures of the artist, Dan Flavin. This 1982 design uses fluorescent tubes in combination with individual halogen lamps in a variety of assemblies suited not only to a wide range of office environments, where both overall and local task lighting is required, but also to the greater demands of, for example, gallery illumination. Electrical connections may be made between the ends of the hanging channels, allowing lighting configurations to be changed without wiring in auxiliary power supplies. Over the years, King and Miranda have designed a number of halogen fixtures – Lucy, Tor, Ra, Alma – that drop from the channels on rods of various lengths.

Another 1982 milestone was the Aurora lamp, an ethereal flying saucer which hovers

Above: After the success of the minimal Jill and Aurora, the Tris Tras lamp, 1986, is evidence of a trend towards more ornate pieces
Opposite: The Triana lamp of 1984 and its wall-mounted companion Murana use glass patterned like that in some of King and Miranda's interiors

become a triple-decker sandwich with a circular plane of methacrylate inserted between the two glass layers. The methacrylate serves to diffuse the light more satisfactorily and all three planes work like the fins of a heat-sink to keep the lamp cool.

During the 1980s, the lamps King and Miranda designed grew more ornate. Triana and its wall-mounted companion, Murana, Palio and Tris Tras provide evidence of the in-roads made by new lighting technology into the home. There was even the ill-fated Pi lamp, commissioned by a British client under the Design Council's funded consultancy scheme. The client company lost its nerve and the Pi was never put into production.

This run culminated in the Gabriel lamp, designed in 1987. Apparently the exact opposite in spirit to the Jill, the Gabriel was turned down by Arteluce, not for the taste in evidence in its rococo form (ironically, Gandini would prefer this lamp in his home to any other of King and Miranda's domestic designs), but because of the expense of the many parts involved in its assembly. Yet there is a kinship with Jill, in that Gabriel once again brings materials more familiar in industry into a domestic setting. Sheet brass is worked in various ways and a low-precision technology is used to achieve a rich and refined effect.

from three wires of equal length, typically over a dining table. Like the Jill, Aurora established a new domestic archetype and has been much imitated; once again, the components are prosaic, ordinary window glass being the principal material. The first version of the Aurora comprised two glass discs with three 50 watt halogen bulbs sandwiched between them. Conceptually attractive, the prototype soon revealed minor faults: the light did not emerge in an ideal fashion and the design trapped heat emitted by the bulbs. The design was modified to

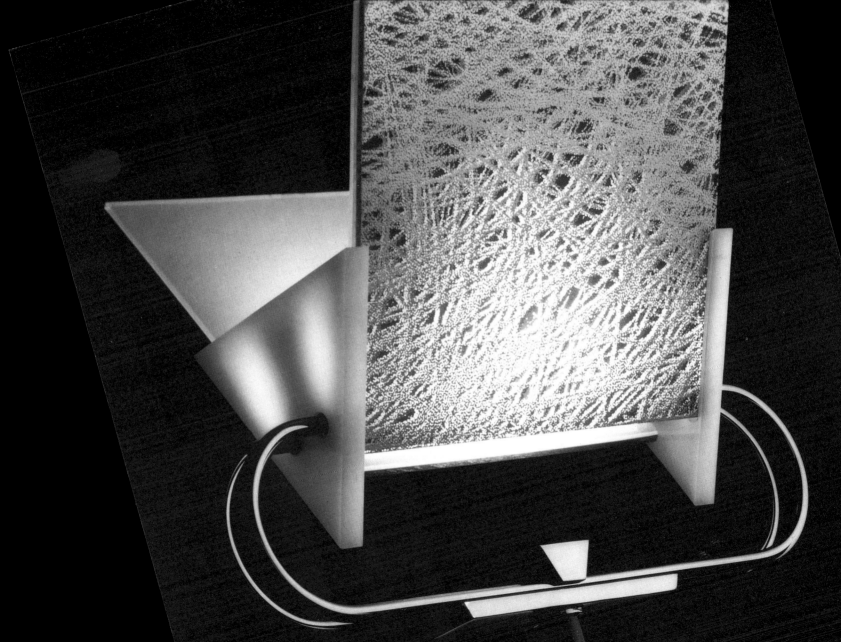

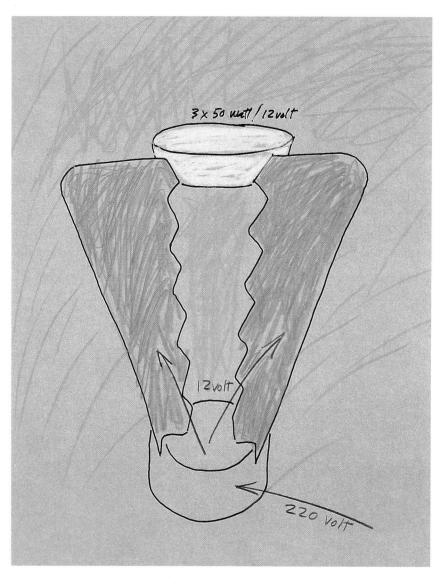

3 × 50 watt / 12 volt

12 volt

220 volt

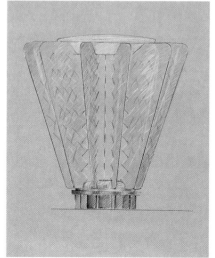

The design for the Gabriel lamp, 1987, evolved through a series of sketches and models, opposite. It was the intention from the beginning to place a transformer in the base and for Gabriel's wings to be live, carrying the 12V supply. The lamp was finished in black nickel-plated steel, right, to maximise the diaphanous effect of the reflection of light from its surfaces

"Gabriel was a deliberate attempt to make something so complex, with individual elements so many and so complicated, that its overall effect would be simple, like a head of hair of a girl that is composed of innumerable strands of hair, yet the overall mass is read as a whole," King explains. "People's interest in objects relies upon an easy reading – you need to get a quick picture. But if this can be enriched with many complex relationships on a smaller scale which the eye and mind can play on later, this is a very positive thing."

Thus the eye is met with a haze of feathery wings, with reflections and transparencies and with reflections of transparencies layered one upon another. "In our design we deliberately used the shadows. We wanted an embroidery: a series of projected forms, avoiding any flattening effect in the illuminated zone. Our grandmothers used to put a doily-mat under their lamps and we wanted to take this idea further and create a 'lace-pattern' on the floor or on the surface where the lamp is placed," wrote Miranda.[2]

The continued prospects for this remarkable *œuvre* may not be so bright. Sergio Gandini thinks creativity may be constrained by the new market conditions in Europe after 1992. More importance will be given to uniformity of quality in products, he feels, and in the short term the need will be for good taste, not radical design. In the longer term, as national cultural identities regain their footing, there will again be room for adventure. Gandini agrees that King and Miranda, with their experience of designing a broad range of products within the strict constraints of international ergonomic standards, are better equipped than most to weather the uncertainty.

As for Arteluce, the aim is to stay small and to retain control over quality rather than to go for quantity at any cost. The strategy is typical of many design-led companies, still family-owned, in both Italy and Spain. Arteluce is leaving nothing to chance and in preparation for greater competition is repositioning its product divisions. In future the structure will comprise Flos and Arteluce, each with its own collection, together with a new brand dedicated to systems lighting for offices. The shift is perhaps the most important in Flos/Arteluce's history. It will enable Arteluce to shed its well-earned but potentially limiting reputation for decorative lighting and will permit each part of the company to innovate with maximum flexibility within its market sector.

The product that will establish the new brand's identity will be the result of four years' work by King and Miranda. Called Sky Light,

the project pulls together many threads explored by the designers in interface design, furniture, interior design and architecture as well as in lighting. Sky Light was presented to Arteluce in 1988, after two years' design work. Once again, the emphasis is on conceptual innovation and technology transfer from one environment to another rather than on new technology *per se*.

It is a sign of the esteem in which King and Miranda are held by their client that the company's initial response to their proposal was to say that it did not have the structure either to develop or to sell the design and from there to set about the necessary restructuring. Entering the decade of the 1990s, it is true to say that Perry King and Santiago Miranda are the legitimate inheritors of Castiglioni and Scarpa.

King and Miranda's most prominent lighting project, however, is nothing to do with either Arteluce or Italy. In 1988, the organisers of the International Expo to be held during 1992 in the Andalucian capital of Seville came to King and Miranda with a commission to design the exterior lighting for the event, one of five major commissions awarded for the design of the Expo site infrastructure. The designers were chosen in part because of recent successes designing

Above: First model in polystyrene foam of the garden lighting bollard for the Seville Expo
Left and right: The Seville Expo park lights use a three-dimensional adaptation of the infinity motif in the form of interlocking discus shapes

For the Seville
Expo street lights,
translucent blue bowls
filter external light,
ensuring that the
overhead lamps have a
decorative role during
daylight hours. When
switched on at night,
far right, the internal
light is visible through
the bowl

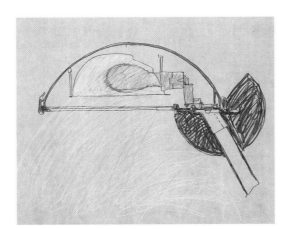

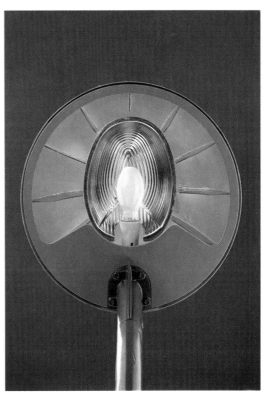

First production
pieces of the park
light designed for
the Seville Expo 1992

Mast lights for the car park and lake of the Expo site will be decorated with illuminated sail-like forms

furniture for Spanish clients, and not least because Seville is the city of Santiago Miranda's birth.

After several months of negotiation, King and Miranda were given the job in February 1989 and presented their designs three months later. Polystyrene models made at the King-Miranda studio were followed by prototypes made in collaboration with Philips External Lighting in France, during which the engineering design was modified.

King and Miranda's designs, done with the help of Malcolm S. Inglis, include street lights, low mushroom-like garden lights, park and car-park lighting and floodlights for buildings – a total of some 10,000 units. Central to the brief was that the lighting should promote Spanish design; after the Expo, it is expected to go into production with Philips in Spain. The designs are based for the most part on a motif that resembles the mathematical symbol for infinity, which in turn is very like the emblem of Seville bequeathed to the city by a king who liberated it from the Arabs in the thirteenth century. The metal structures are to be painted cobalt blue and the street lights will have blue glass bowls giving them a visual interest during daylight as sunlight filters through them, as well as after dark.

The one very different lighting design is

the 35-metre floodlight mast which has a battery of conventional floodlights clustered at its top. King and Miranda's special touch was to add an asymmetric, sculptural white sail which soars above all this, catching and reflecting light beamed skyward that would otherwise be wasted. Three such forms will rise on tall poles in the lake that is a central feature of the site, caravels recalling the voyages of discovery that have set sail from Spain down the centuries. In what will be its quincentenary year, it is entertaining to note that it has taken a Spanish designer based in Italy to evoke an image of one specific voyage, that of the Italian navigator Cristoforo Colombo, who with Spanish funding set forth with his fleet of three ships to discover the New World.

1. J. Dolce, "Four Designers", *International Design*, January/February 1989, pp.52-9.
2. Quoted in M. Romanelli, "La Lampada Gabriel per Arteluce", *Domus*, September 1987, pp.108-9.

King and Miranda established their reputation as furniture designers through their relation–ship with Marcatré, a company whose origins are closely linked with Cassina, one of Italy's most respected furniture manufacturers, whose founder, Cesare Cassina, was in the vanguard of efforts to modernise Italian design after the Second World War. First through the architect Gio Ponti and later with younger figures such as Gaetano Pesce and Afra and Tobia Scarpa, Cassina built up a reputation for leadership in domestic furniture.

In the mid-1970s, Cassina's director Rodrigo Rodriguez established Marcatré in order to break into the lucrative office furniture market. Piero Portoghese became its president. "Rodriguez was astute enough to understand that it wasn't a matter of building up a division for office furniture inside Cassina," he says, "but of starting a completely new venture." Other Italian companies were also coming round to the idea of selling office furniture, muscling in on a market that had been dominated by just one manufacturer, Tecno, with its Graphis product. But the transition to manufacturing for the two different markets was not a simple one. It was a mistake to think that the office product, its buyers and its distribution were essentially the same as for the domestic product. Another was to assume that the office market was ready for the same degree of sophistication seen in Italian domestic furniture during the previous decades.

Rodriguez foresaw these pitfalls, but Marcatré's début was nevertheless not an easy one. Marcatré's advantage was its access, through Cassina, to the best designers – Mario Bellini and Paolo Deganello and other members of the Archizoom group were among the first to be approached. But there were problems in setting up the high-volume industrial production line that would be needed in place of the largely manual, batch assembly and craft finishing processes used for domestic furniture. These difficulties coincided with the impact of the 1973 oil crisis and a general downturn in demand for office space and accessories.

It was into this unpromising commercial atmosphere that King and Miranda dropped the results of their Unlimited Horizon research studies into the nature of work and its relationship with furniture one day back in 1978. The connection with Marcatré was established at a dinner party in Milan , which in turn led to an invitation to talk about the possiblities of working together.

A typically overwhelming King-Miranda presentation, Unlimited Horizon began as a chart of furniture types plotted against environment types. Where there was a need for one type of furniture in a particular setting, the designers entered a black spot in the appropriate box on the chart. For each spot, King and Miranda had designed the requisite piece of furniture – over two hundred pieces in all, representing more than a year's work. This was no theoretical project, though the designers knew they would be lucky to see the tiniest fraction of the total *œuvre* go into production. King prefers to describe it as a practical project without a conclusion. "We were not interested in being paper architects. Its use has been to inform projects since."

To this day, the Unlimited Horizon studies have not been published. Had they been intended merely as "paper architecture", they surely would have been long ago. King and Miranda are doubly coy about the work now, since some of it bears a remarkable likeness, in its use of colour, texture patterns and chunky solid forms, to the furniture of the Memphis movement. Unlimited Horizon predates any Memphis announcement, but King and Miranda would be foolish to hope that its retrospective publication would prove their point. Nevertheless, Unlimited Horizon does share some of Memphis's goals, if not its polemical method. "Our objectives were the

same – to renew the modern without falling into that certain moral self-satisfaction that existed in the Modern Movement. We've never wanted to design things whose only function was a publicity function for the company that ordered them."

Portoghese was stunned by the work, but at that time was in no position to support its further development. "It would have offered a huge spectrum of possibilities, but I remember that I had to say very frankly that we had no interest at that moment. We had other troubles to solve and were not ready for something of this magnitude." King and Miranda went away disappointed, but in truth knowing what they had suspected all along.

It was not until a year or so later that Portoghese called. By then he had positioned Marcatré to his satisfaction as a specialist in office furniture, had equipped himself with a new factory in Misinto, north of Milan, and had established a direction for his company. Marcatré already had a number of desk ranges, to which King and Miranda would in due course add their own contribution. But Portoghese's priority now was a range of chairs that would complement the rest of the furniture.

The initial brief was for a range of chairs for different tasks to accompany the Bellini

Il Pianeta Ufficio office system furniture, now more than fifteen years old, which was Marcatré's staple product. Bellini's desks were designed as a universal system applicable at all levels in the office hierarchy. For their chairs, however, King and Miranda decided to avoid the formal similarity of a family of products, a shrewd judgment that would later permit them greatly to broaden the visual vocabulary of the Marcatré range and eventually to add to it a number of highly individual chairs for occasional use.

Designers and client worked together to balance the marketing requirement that the chairs should share characteristics with the need to ensure their suitability to particular and quite different tasks. The designers made polystyrene models to refine the form of each version before briefly taking on a design engineer to finalise the adjustment mechanism and other details. The development work then moved to Marcatré's technical department. In collaboration with Annibale Mandelli, an engineer who had worked at Olivetti on products by Bellini and Sottsass, they made more detailed models before going into prototyping.

Mandelli praises King and Miranda's thoroughness. Their proposals, he says, tend to be both more precise and more realistic than others', which makes them easier to work with than other designers. Though they are not the worst offenders by any means, Mandelli found that King and Miranda could err on the side of seeming precision. "Mandelli was critical of some of the details. He feels that designers have a 'watchmaking' tendency in their approach to engineering – concealed details are made to look beautiful on the drawing-board when what matters ultimately is that the mechanism of an adjustable office seat such as Air Mail is strong, low-cost, easily cast and machined and that components will cause no anxiety in use.

Right and opposite: The characteristic feature of all the 1981 Air Mail chairs is the boomerang shape to the backrest, the result of breaking with ergonomics conventions and attempting to cater for people who sit incorrectly as well as correctly

Mandelli felt that the chair could become too expensive.... The original base consisted of too many parts, the curves of the armrests were too compounded for easy making, the seat mechanism was too complex and possibly not as strong as it could be."[1]

It is nevertheless to King and Miranda's as well as Mandelli's credit that despite these structural and functional modifications, the Air Mail range emerged looking essentially as the designers had rendered it in their early presentations. The area of greatest compromise was the base unit for the swivelling models, in which the gracefully arched feet proposed were replaced by comparatively ill-detailed angular feet. The principal unifying characteristic of all the seating is a functional one. Taking their cue from the Swedish ergonomist, Bengt Åkerblom,[2] King and Miranda designed each chair to allow for a range of seated positions. These included not only the one ergonomically approved position, but also – and this was the heart of the innovation – some of the infinite range of incorrect positions that people will inevitably adopt from time to time. When it was conceived, Air Mail was one of the earliest attempts to escape from the confines of the chair as a machine for sitting in, with a battery of control mechanisms that allowed for people of different shapes but only conceded one "right" way of sitting. In the event, however, the Air Mail chairs took so long to come on to the market that several other manufacturers released similar products first.

King and Miranda's initial proposals met with huge resistance, in particular as Marcatré's technical support was still insufficient to cope with what were seen as unnecessary complications. The designers proposed a chair that would provide good lumbar support for task work, but could be adapted when required to provide equally good back support in a relaxed, leaning position. Both positions are likely ones for a manager who works sometimes alone at a terminal but who also breaks off for discussions with colleagues. The back-tilt mechanism was to be operated by a lever positioned at the point where the backrest would pivot, while the seat height would be adjusted in the conventional manner by a control lever under the seat.

Marcatré resisted placing the back-tilt lever at the rear of the chair. It felt that it was too small a company to force such a new expectation on a market accustomed to finding adjustment mechanisms under the seat, and in tests, people had found reaching for the lever uncomfortable. King and Miranda lost this battle and the Air Mail chair as manufactured has two levers slung under the seat, one on the right and one on the left. Putting the levers here simplified the engineering, but left the possibility that the user would confuse the two controls.

Marcatré's literature today lists more than forty variants of Air Mail, divided into five basic types – a fixed chair, a non-specialist task chair, a typist's chair, and the more recent additions of an advanced task chair and management chair. The variations stem from the fact that many of the chairs are available with different bases and with or without armrests. There is a multiple version for use in waiting-rooms and similar environments, as well as permutations of finishes – with cloth or leather upholstery – and of colours. King and Miranda even designed the fabric, a homely, speckled cloth appropriately called Cardigan.

The basic models have plastic armrests, each with its tip bevelled at an angle, the compromise reached after the designers' more sculptural curved detail was found too complex to mould. This surface provides comfortable arm positioning for office workers using VDUs, as well as a distinctive visual element at the low end of the range. The only property shared by virtually the entire range is the distinctive sharp bend of the backrest, the product of that wish to provide strong lumbar support while the user is sitting up, as well as comfort while leaning back.

For the advanced task versions, Marcatré at first asked simply for a variety of backrests, with different heights signifying different levels of authority. This marketing ploy would have provided the appearance of product differentiation without loss of economy of scale as the backrests would simply bolt on to the same basic chair. But King and Miranda insisted on a more rigorous approach. The high-backed version, they reasoned, might belong to a manager who would rarely use a computer. So they modified the design by narrowing the backrest, introducing flexible flaps hidden under the leather upholstery to allow for free shoulder movement. Portoghese was exasperated because the now substantial modification meant more work for his technical staff. However, he could not deny the attraction of the idea.

Portoghese recognises the need for innovation in his products, but talks about it in measured terms. "The degree of freedom which you can have in domestic furniture or in lighting, for example, is much wider than in office furniture. When you buy something for yourself you are free to buy what you want.

The poster for the
Air Mail chair, part
of a series of graphic
material produced for
Marcatré between 1982
and 1986, is printed
on flimsy air mail
type paper

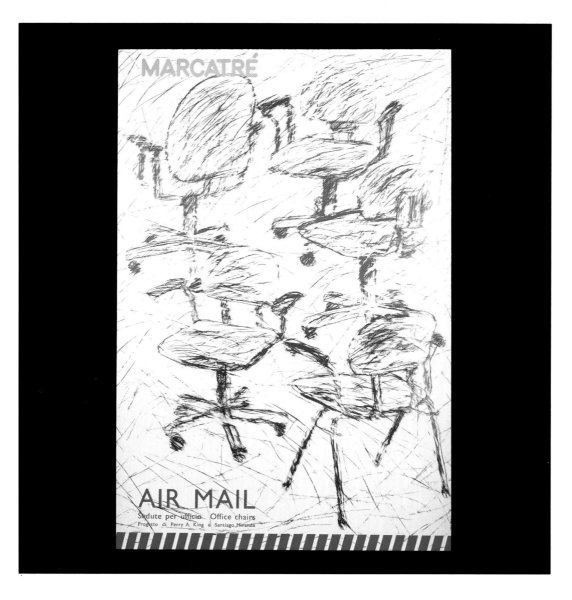

Above: Air Mail chairs can be joined together for use in waiting areas

make sound business sense too. It all sounds very much like the stereotypical situation of designer and client in a country accustomed to less enlightened design patronage, such as Britain or the United States. But even in Italy, creativity in design has to square with commercial ambitions with all the tensions that this implies. On occasion sharp differences in opinion have even resulted in a product being dropped; in 1986, for example, work was discontinued after prototypes had been made for a secretarial table by King and Miranda because its design was considered "too rich" for the market.

But buyers for offices have a responsibility to the users, so it is inappropriate for them to express their own tastes too strongly. On the other hand, the architects and the specifiers are looking for innovation in the furniture that they use, and we want to interest them too, but the balance has to be very carefully tuned."

King and Miranda's relationship with Marcatré mirrors this unstable balance precisely. They tend to push for radical solutions, but their clients are not always convinced. According to King and Miranda, radical attitudes need not mean just risky innovation for innovation's sake, but can also

Building on the catalogue of product types laid out in the Unlimited Horizon project, King and Miranda have wanted to add new products to Marcatré's range. Their only companion desk to the Air Mail seating was the basic Cable, designed in 1983. At the top end of the range, Marcatré had Castiglioni's masterful Solone desk and its related components. But there was nothing in between to suit the new management roles anticipated by the more advanced Air Mail chairs. King and Miranda had been working on a thorough update for Cable, but in 1989 the project was put on hold as the new executive chairs were seen as a more marketable priority. Marcatré's

Right: Cable, 1983, is King and Miranda's uncontroversial range of tables for Marcatré
Opposite: The Air Mail Visitor's Chair, 1987, while visually lightweight, is unusually heavy as the result of a compromise between the design specification and manufacturing capability

interim solution was Carini's rather conservative Zelig desk system. Their own desk designs, say King and Miranda, would have benefited from their knowledge of the science and psychology of the high-tech interface gained while working on the Experimental Personal Office Computer for Olivetti. This experience is yet to be exploited in a practical design project for Marcatré, although the company's larger rivals both in Italy and elsewhere are increasingly teaming up with computer manufacturers in an effort to integrate the design of desks and computers.

Over the years, King and Miranda have grown more playful with their client. Laying the groundwork for the presentation of the later executive chairs in the Air Mail range, for example, they used movie stills of men in suits to depict the risibility of middle-management life – the Marx Brothers, Doctor Strangelove, Fred Astaire dancing on the ceiling. It was an invitation to think about clerical work as it is and as it could be if its pretentious seriousness were leavened with a little humour. The first of the new generation of Air Mail chairs, the Visitor's Chair, is evidence of this new spirit. It is markedly more adventurous than its predecessors, with a quality of suspended animation – not the windblown look of Massimo Iosa-Ghini and his fellow Bolidists with their streamlined chairs and tables, but a poised appearance of frozen motion, like that of an animal about to pounce on its prey. "We're very interested in a chair that lifts its heels, that has grace, that's light on its feet. But it's essentially static – you're the person who moves on the chair – and the idea of a streamlined chair is a bit ridiculous."

The rear legs of the Visitor's Chair are ramrod straight, the forelegs gracefully arched. The lateral connection between the two pairs of legs is by means of two chrome-plated steel tubes, the ends of which are joined at each side of the chair, not entirely satisfactorily, by a

boomerang-shaped metal plate. The interest in this feature is that the curve of the plate is not aligned with the curve of the front leg. This makes it look as if the chair frame is hinged at the point where the two arcs join, so the weight of the chair appears to reach the ground in two hops. The detailing is not perfect, and the overall design is distinctly heavy, physically if not visually. King and Miranda put this down to having to over-engineer parts of the chair to overcome technical limitations. In particular, their proposal for the seat attachment to the frame called for an aluminium casting which proved unacceptable to the client.

The Visitor's Chair was quite a departure for Marcatré, but it proved to be only a softening-up exercise in King and Miranda's terms. The latest prototypes, a director's chair called Dirigenziale and a complex upholstered conference chair called Vestita, are sufficiently different that they may not even be marketed as part of the Air Mail range. They represent something of a victory for King and Miranda, considerably stretching Marcatré's design language, but they could also yet prove a huge coup for Marcatré itself as it moves into a segment of the seating market where more individuality is acceptable.

Five years into what had been an exclusive

The Vestita conference chair, above, and Dirigenziale director's chair, right, of 1989 are the latest additions to the Air Mail range and the least compromised of King and Miranda's designs for Marcatré

relationship with Marcatré (that is, the designers worked only for this furniture client), King and Miranda began making overtures to and responding to invitations from other furniture companies, not only in Italy but also in Spain. It is tempting to see this renewed interest in Spanish clients as a congenial if uncommercial diversion from the constraints of mainstream jobs. This would be misleading, however. All the new furniture is destined for markets very different from those pursued by Marcatré and much of it is manufactured in low-tech, low-volume factories.

King and Miranda's re-entry into Spain after the Norma Europa débâcle began with Disform. Of the many manufacturers leading the current renaissance in Spanish design, Disform is probably the best known, largely for its association with the French design superstar, Philippe Starck. King and Miranda had met Carlos Riera of Disform while the Norma Europa project was under way, eight years earlier. They had grown to like him and his do-it-yourself determination to spread good design in Spain, come what may. King and Miranda designed two collections for Disform – the theatrical and blatantly post-modern. Gongora shelf and Tibi Dabo storage unit of 1985 and the Beato chairs

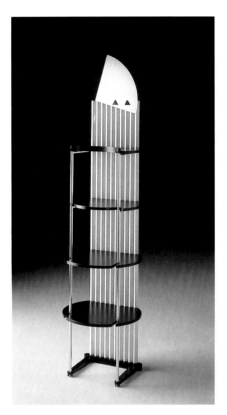

Disform was King
and Miranda's first
productive Spanish
client. The Tibi Dabo
storage unit, 1985,
was a product of a
shortlived collaboration

and sofas of the following year, a disjointed assemblage of black metal frame with a cloth-upholstered seat, leather armrests and a draped, quilted back hanging down behind like a roll of carpet, each surface a different colour, pattern or texture.

But King and Miranda were soon to discover that Riera's *ad hoc* approach had disadvantages as well as advantages and they turned their attention to Akaba. A tiny company with a total of five people in its offices near San Sebastian, Akaba has little money but a burning desire to make a mark through good, adventurous design. "We thought this was an interesting challenge. What they needed was something that would be noticed, but they had a complete inability to make anything or to make any kind of investment."

Since Akaba was obviously unable to fabricate complex structural components, King and Miranda decided to incorporate ready-made parts into their designs. For the legs of the La Vuelta desks and tables they used bicycle forks, readily available from a local cycle-parts manufacturer, though expediency was far from the only reason for the choice. Bicycling is popular with many Spaniards – not least Santiago Miranda – and so the La Vuelta furniture would signal its

cultural kinship. The voluptuous shape of the desk and table legs is enhanced by means of a curved metal rod which provides a structural counterpoint to the bicycle fork. The witty device carries historical echoes of past styles in wooden furniture, as well as an unavoidable reference to Marcel Duchamp. And the design got the company the attention it craved. As one French journal remarked humorously: "There has been until now no *rapport* between the bicycle and the table, certainly not from the point of view of function, nor in terms of dynamism or lightness of line. Nothing unites the two if not the 'spoken' language which

The use of bicycle front forks as part of the leg construction of the La Vuelta tables of 1986, shown here as prototypes, brought Spanish manufacturer Akaba the media attention it craved

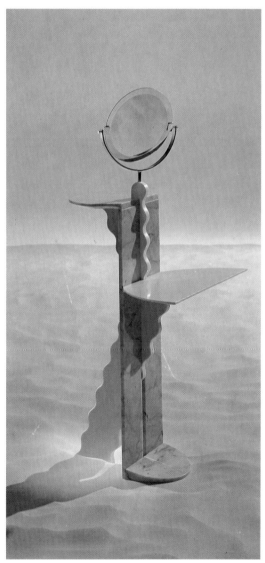

The marriage of traditional crafts with contemporary design is exemplified in the Altipiani marble tables for Lombardi Project, 1988. Their homage to the Surrealists is made explicit in the photography

Opposite: The Bloom bookshelf for T70, 1988, is simple but elegant in its modular assembly

associates by means of metaphor the vocabulary of the cyclist with that of the bureaucrat when forced to summon a great effort: *en piste, pédaler*, etc."[3]

A more recent piece for the rather more traditional and long-established company Andreu Est in Valencia is the 1990 Soleá chair, a locust-like animal that once again reworks the theme of suspended animation, but this time in wood. Like any zoomorphic wooden chair made in Spain, the nod to Antoni Gaudí is inescapable. For Italian clients, too, there have been since 1988 sporadic releases of designs very different in character from the work for Marcatré. Nothing could be further removed from the office environment than the Altipiani series of marble tables for Lombardi Project, evocatively named after French authors (Marguerite D., Marcel P.) and photographed in a style inspired by the paintings of Salvador Dalí.

The game of literary charades is continued in the Bloom bookshelf, one of a series of products for T70, a little-known manufacturer of wardrobes and domestic cabinets. With its policy of good design at good prices, T70 is conspicuously less élitist than, say, B&B or Cassina. It is now struggling to expand its range, but lacks the necessary manufacturing flexibility. The Bloom shelf and ingenious

Pitagoro table, which conceals in its legs a support that allows it to be extended, are the first products to emerge from this collaboration. But the elegant, low-cost Esperona chair, shown at the 1988 Milan Furniture Fair, will probably not be manufactured by T70, and a subsequent range of beds and night-tables looks likely to go the same way.

Rather more successful is King and Miranda's first product for the American company Atelier International, now part of the rapidly expanding empire of Steelcase, the world's largest office furniture manufacturer. Commissioned late in 1989, the piece is essentially a simple metal-framed side chair with variants with or without arms and the option of a sled-base as an alternative to legs. It is less outrageous than, say, the Beato chairs, but by American standards it is very unusual. The black, upholstered backrest that resembles nothing more than a cocked hat – on the one hand, a transparent pastiche of European motifs (a bull's head or the tricorne of Napoleon or Nelson) and on the other, an American *hommage* – George Washington was a potential name.

King and Miranda entertain ambitions that their work for Atelier International will open doors to larger commissions for Steelcase.

The Esperona chair
of 1988, originally
designed for T70
but unlikely now to
go into production,
continues the theme
of suspended
animation first
articulated in the Air
Mail Visitor's Chair

King and Miranda called
their first piece for
American client Atelier
International the
N Chair, an oblique
reference to the
Napoleonic tricorne
backrest

The Pitagoro
(Pythagoras) table,
designed in 1988 for
T70, houses a bracket
in each leg to support
drop-leaves

Meanwhile Mercatré, for all the nuances of the relationship, remains their most consistent client. Though friction can undoubtedly help the creative process along, it can also bring frustrations and disagreements. King and Miranda are hardly confrontational types and they prefer design to politics, but they make no secret that they would like to have taken some of their designs further than has proved possible.

Certainly their association with Marcatré has coincided with a period of sustained growth for the company, and an exponential jump in their own international reputation. But despite the occasional tensions, progress has been made, with the designer influencing client and client influencing designer. When one considers that the earliest Air Mail chairs were contemporary with the highly refined Expanded Line lighting system – also intended for office use – it is clear that the most recent King and Miranda designed furniture is much closer to the direction that their work is taking in other areas.

There is a more concrete indication that this particular creative partnership can bear fruit in the stunning series of interiors the designers have created for Marcatré's showrooms around the world. These serve as a demonstration of the company's potential as a force for creative design. Given their head, King and Miranda have risen to the challenge of creating work that is appropriate both in poetic expression and in response to very real constraints of budget, market and context. They are a constant reassurance, too, to King and Miranda that there is a creative reward for their perseverance.

1. J. Glancey, "High-Flier from Milan", *The Architectural Review*, May 1985, pp.53-7.
2. Åkerblom, "Anatomische und Physiologische Grundlagen zur Gestaltung von Sitzen" in *Sitting Posture* (ed. E. Grandjean), Taylor and Francis, London 1976.
3. "Vuelta Tables", *L'Architecture d'Aujourd'hui*, April 1988, p.88.

King and Miranda have over the years designed all of Marcatré's major showrooms in Italy and the rest of Europe. Freed from the constrictions of having to come up with designs that the company is sure it will be able to sell, they have been able to indulge their decorative tastes and their predilection for the allusive and narrative to the full. Perry King believes that the courage Marcatré shows in commissioning showrooms stems from the company's belief that architectural patronage provides an opportunity to make a bold statement about the company's view of design. Designing the showrooms in which Marcatré's staff conduct their business gave King the chance to produce a more radical kind of design than would be appropriate for the company's general product range. To King, the showrooms are not peripheral; rather, they are an essential part of creating an identity through which clients can communicate their message.

Each showroom represents a response to its particular city. There is no corporate identity as such, though the designers' signature is immediately apparent in each space, providing a unifying thread and contributing to the creation of an image now recognisable as "Marcatré" within the industry. King and Miranda's sense of the need to provide an identity, however oblique, stems perhaps from

their professional backgrounds. "Since they come from graphics and industry rather than from purely architectural backgrounds, their work has unceasingly been directed towards the constant and coherent development of what we can safely call a corporate image, in the very best sense of the term," writes Gillo Dorfles of their work in general,[1] an observation nowhere more true than of the showrooms.

The first showroom, opened in 1981, was on a little street known for its artists' studios in Rome. Federico Fellini reportedly lived above the site. King and Miranda's idea was to infer an office environment from a few clues. Being in Rome, they could not resist giving the showroom a pseudo-archaeological air. In one of the offbeat parables they are wont to produce for each interior project, King and Miranda wrote of the putative archaeological site guides who would point out the paved roads, the forum, the peristyles and so on with "a superb indifference to our inability to 'see' [them] … our inexpert eye could only see a certain unevenness in the land or at most a few vaguely geometrically shaped stones. But the guides … stooped and lifted the tarpaulin when we least expected it and there it was – the mosaic.

"They, the guides, knew very well that

In Marcatré's Rome showroom, 1981, thousands of chopped electrical insulation filaments sprout from the panels that delineate the display space

from then on they had won … and gradually we would begin, from that mosaic, to 'see' the colonnade, the basilica, the walls and the fountains."[2]

In the Rome showroom, a perimeter rim of blue symbolises the sky, enhancing the feeling of being in the open air at a dig. Some of the walls are covered, not with classical frescoes and mosaics, but with patterns from printed circuit boards. King and Miranda carved out a "road", which runs diagonally from the entrance to the back of the room, by means of the "slight unevenness" of a change in the marble floor slabs from grey to white. The use of the diagonal makes it look from the street as if you are facing into the corner of a room, implying that the missing half extends out on to the pavement to enclose the onlooker. In effect, King and Miranda's archaeological fragments lay a new stratum over the floorplan of the existing building, skewed at an angle from that plan as surely as the building itself is skewed from the Roman remains that lie somewhere below.

King and Miranda are not afraid to mix metaphors, and the archaeological theme is not the only one present. The walls that divide up the display spaces, reaching not quite to the ceiling nor quite stretching to the next panel, are thought of as screens behind which

Opposite and right:
The plan of the Rome
showroom is on a grid
set at 45 degrees to the
building plan,
giving scope for
archaeological jokes.
Contrasting stone
finishes are used to
suggest paths across
the space, while
illuminated blue panels
overhead introduce an
open-air feeling

indicating that it will shortly pass. In much the same way, King and Miranda's interior contains many points where one stands in foreboding gloom, but can see a brighter promise on the horizon.

The flirtatiousness with which King and Miranda gradually reveal one space from another is a trade-mark of their showrooms, as is the carefully judged exposure to any sample office environment. "It's very important in a furniture showroom that the office space is accessible visually, but it should not be too close – a real, working office almost always looks rather squalid," King points out.

King and Miranda deployed many similar effects in their first job in Japan, for the design of a discothèque, Sogno A, in 1984. Here rich materials such as marble, slate and slabs of silk-screened printed glass give a suggestion of permanence in a fleeting environment. "The 'Sogno A' invokes far distant times, both past and future, and draws its potency as an image from the contrast," wrote one critic. "It's like being inside some very posh primeval spacecraft."[3]

Since their début in interior design with the Rome showroom, King and Miranda had been creating Marcatré's exhibition stands at each year's EIMU, the Esposizione Internazionale Mobili Ufficio in Milan. Their

a beautiful woman might be changing. In fact, of course, Marcatré's furniture stands in for this tantalising prospect. Where the walls break to provide glimpses from one space to another, the break is softened with a moustache of thousands of bright blue electrical insulation wires bristling into the vertical slot. Dangling in space, forever waiting for connection into some non-existent network, the wires are a symbol of the diffused communications in the office of the future. The lighting was inspired by a Turner watercolour depicting a storm about to burst, but with a band of blue in the distance

second permanent showroom for the company was in Turin, to be followed by ones in Milan, Pisa and Genoa as well as an impressive office for Cassina in Tokyo in 1985, and by Bologna, London, and a short-lived Glasgow office the following year.

Milan is the undisputed capital of Italian furniture design and any Italian manufacturer's showroom here will be seen as its flagship. In collaboration with architect Renata Fusi, King and Miranda rose to this daunting challenge not by pouring in a flood of allusions and references, but by exercising restraint. The overwhelming first impression of the Milan showroom is one of greyness. Its subtle array of tones and textures echoes the sombre Milan streets, where buildings are grander and greyer than those of most Italian cities.

The space is a simple, two-storey shoe-box. The street frontage is fairly narrow, and this section runs through to the back of the showroom, where a white marble staircase spirals up round a pair of slim black columns. Ceilings and columns are a *faux* grey marble created by a traditional Venetian treatment using powdered marble in plaster applied *spatolato* for uneven coloration, then waxed to seem like polished stone. The walls are made up of printed panels decorated with a coarse shading of magnified pencil fleck marks, grey once again but more coarsely textured than other surfaces. Metal mesh screens along part of the back wall hide building services and continue the grey theme with yet another textural variation. The floors are rectangular slabs of alternating coarse- and fine-grained Lombardy granite as used traditionally in opulent Milanese *palazzi*.

The narrative behind the design, for what it is worth, concerns the entry to the Forbidden City in Beijing. The design is intended to express a symbolic hierarchy, as in the sequence of spaces leading to the Imperial Palace, an effect spoiled somewhat by the way the street entrance has been altered since 1985. As originally envisaged, the showroom window was set back from the line of the other stores along the Via Manzoni. From the shallow threshold of white marble that originally made the transition from the public pavement to the interior, a composite column of four slim black pillars rises up to the ground-floor ceiling level and beyond. This feature is now diminished, sandwiched as it is between the new outer and the old inner showroom windows. The visitor then runs the gauntlet of grey granite on the ground-floor show space, with the white stairs at the rear beckoning to the upper floor. Journey's end is an enigmatic cube of white light supported on the black entrance columns,

now framed in the centre of the first-floor street window.

One of the distinguishing features of King and Miranda's interiors lies in their ability to create a startling effect with scant resources. This talent was to be tested to the limit in London, a project executed with the help of Carlos Moya and Maria Castro in Milan and Robin Derrick in London. Never the biggest spender on design generally or on contract furniture, London did not warrant a large budget in the first place. And as much of what money there was had already been spent on a scheme that had come to grief, the interior that did emerge was squeezed for cash indeed. It is the only one not to be treated to a custom-designed lamp, for example, using off-the-peg Arteluce Lucy, Ra and Expanded Line lighting. In addition, the London property doubles up to display not only Marcatré furniture, but also work from Cassina and lighting from Flos/Arteluce. Robert Webster, formerly Marcatré's managing director in Britain, reveals the essential conservatism. "When we did that showroom it was quite a brave thing. At the end of the day here, we're selling office furniture against Herman Miller and Steelcase, and yet we made the showroom completely avant-garde."

Like Rome and Milan, this showroom

reflects certain qualities of the city that surrounds it. London's flat northern light, very different from the harsh sunlit contrasts of Italy, finds its echo in the pale wash of the main display space. The lighting is more even than in the other showrooms and the grey marble, which in Italy provides a welcoming cool darkness, is here exchanged for a warm wooden floor, little more exotic by a random flecked texture of pale ash and darker iroko fillets. King and Miranda place great importance on the floor, against which, after all, any piece of furniture will be judged. A touch of inexpensive drama is provided by screens in a reflective silvery fabric that may be hung from the ceiling to create a sanctum around a chosen article of furniture. Sadly, the screens are seldom in evidence.

The space is given its signature by a triptych of wall drawings in King and Miranda's inimitable style. These allude to three communication activities mentioned in a preamble to the designers' most ambitious discourse on an interior. "Few human activities have aroused less enthusiam in our collective imagination than office work," they write. "Very few young people will have dreamt on a midsummer's night of a safe job in an office … while the jobs available in industry decrease every day, the possibility of writing, talking and reading – of communicating – in the office increases.… We believe that few places can be compared, for the potential capacity of interactive communication, to a modern office equipped with those productivity tools, in no way futuristic, that are available today."[4]

There was much discussion about King and Miranda's proposals for the murals, which depict in a romanticised way the spread of information from hand to page, from mouth to ear, and from page to eye involved in writing, talking and reading. Unlike most of the showroom details, the concept required the approval not only of Webster but also of

The London showroom
of 1985-86 was on a
tight budget. Silver
screens, above, and
sketch murals, left,
provide the distinctive
King and Miranda –
and hence Marcatré –
signature

Portoghese. "There were a lot of discussions about the actual art on the walls," Webster recalls. "I felt that we'd gone so far with the thoughts behind the design that we had to allow them to complete the design in their own way. I think that was probably the bravest thing that we did. I suppose the worry about it is that we are an office furniture showroom; are we taking it too far? Perry convinced me it was part of what we should be doing. Perry was very good at selling the concept and very insistent upon not compromising."

The humanistic vision of office life revealed in the murals shows the continuity between King and Miranda's experience of man-machine interfaces at Olivetti and their thinking about interior design. In both cases, their commentary is made graphically. The process by which a user interprets the symbols on an Olivetti photocopier panel is essentially the same as that whereby a showroom visitor decodes the wall drawings. In both cases, the images are elliptical enough to allow for a wide variety of personal readings, or even no reading at all. Whatever the interpretation, the higher demands of the function of the equipment or the space are in no way impaired. Any fears Webster might have had turned out to be ill founded; most contract buyers fail to notice the murals, or at least fail

to comment upon them. Visiting architects and designers, on the other hand, often praise them.

There is no evidence of the trepidation shown in London in the design for the Paris showroom, completed in 1989 and without doubt the boldest and richest yet. Unlike London, but like the Bologna showroom that immediately preceded it, the Paris project was comparatively well funded, with a total budget of about £200,000. The site is a modern building with a Portland stone and bronze facade, located on the Avenue Hoch just down the hill from the Arc de Triomphe. The ground-floor showroom presents a sheer glass wall to the street, making it hard, particularly on a bright day, to see past the reflections on the glass. Perseverance is rewarded, however, for to glimpse the interior from this vantage-point is to stare back half a millennium into the landscapes of the Renaissance.

There is no hint in this view of the remarkably awkward sequence of spaces that runs back from the display window, dodging around the building's lobby space and a small courtyard garden. Working once again in collaboration with Carlos Moya, King and Miranda opted not to unify this unruly hodgepodge of rooms, but rather to give each its own distinctive décor, lighting and mood.

Above and opposite: The showroom in Bologna soon joined the principal Marcatré showrooms in Rome and Milan

They abandoned the main entrance off the street, both to maximise the window space and in acknowledgment of the fact that this was to be a showroom, not a shop depending on passing trade. The display window remained blocked by an internal structural column practically up against it, however. Unable to remove it, the designers chose instead to disguise it as a mysterious astronomical measuring device. This mystical semicircular object, apparently of bronze but in fact of fibreglass, hangs in mid-air, tantalisingly not quite in contact with the window. The designers say it is based on an inscribed monument in Jaipur, and the inscriptions are doubtless as mysterious as the ones in India, with hints of alphabetic lettering, or perhaps computer numerals, or electronic symbols.

Behind this runic tablet, a number of marble slabs are set into the floor in a radial pattern as if to measure the passing of the hours from the shadow it casts on a sunny day. And beyond this begins the showroom proper. The first of its spaces is a passage too narrow to display more than one large object, such as a Castiglioni table. This is no bad thing in effect, but in order to make it appear that a grand space has been purposely contracted as if by screens to heighten the presence of the displayed object, the designers have placed

mirrors along the two parallel long walls from head-height to the ceiling, so that the lower parts of the walls appear to be temporary partitions. The walls themselves are finished with panels that have a silk-screened silver decoration which changes colour as you walk past. This too is intended to convey a feeling that the space you are walking through is bigger than it really is.

The *coup de grâce* here was to deck the ceiling with golden clouds, improbably made of the steel wool used to scour frying-pans. Shafts of light shine down from the Lucy lamps through and around these clouds, bouncing misty reflections from the wall panels. The combination of light from beneath and behind the clouds gives them the appearance of hanging, while also reminding you that they must be heavier than air, ethereally suspended with the same lack of realism as in a *cinquecento* painting. The clouds too are reflected by the mirrors to infinity and the unlimited horizon.

Behind all the golden fleece is a cerulean ceiling, an echo of the open-air effect in the Rome showroom as well as a continuation of a long tradition of painting ceilings blue and gold that stretches from Greek temples to the Renaissance and, thanks to classical revivalism, to the present. The space might appear like a painting from the early Renaissance – Paolo Uccello or Piero della Francesca – or from the Surrealist brush of de Chirico. King and Miranda's tale this time concerns the Seville-born painter Velázquez, however. As usual, the execution of the project closely resembles the initial conception presented to Yann Thomas, Marcatré's director in Paris. Surprisingly, only the golden clouds were a late addition.

Though the smallest, this room is by far the strongest part of the project. The main space lies to the rear, with a window on to the garden on one side. The area is low-ceilinged and a number of columns interrupt the space. Once again making a virtue of a necessity, King and Miranda have added rows of columns of their own, making the room into a veritable hypostyle.

The striped blue and white columns are clad in frosted glass lit from within. The combination of their bluish glow and the standard overhead fluorescent tubes casts a harsh, cold light. The space is temporarily used as offices but the crypt-like setting will eventually house the systems furniture, leaving the front space free for the showpieces. Marcatré sees this segregation as an important way of delineating activities in a company once known for its systems furniture, but now adding more individual pieces to its inventory.

Right: King and
Miranda's most
arresting Marcatré
showroom, designed
in 1989, is in Paris.
From the outside, the
passer-by is intrigued
by the enigmatic script
on the tablet that
divides the display
window
Overleaf: Golden steel-
wool clouds appear
in frosted patches of
glass in the doorway
between the front and
rear showrooms

Opposite: The drama of the main Paris display space works best when given over to a single centrepiece such as this Castiglioni table
Right: Striped blue and white columns and fluorescent lighting give a cooler appearance to the secondary display space, intended for systems furniture

Esperona Vestita, mixed media on paper, 200 x 146cm, is one of several retrospective paintings created for the 1990 "Lonely Tools" exhibition

Between these two display spaces is a central hub, and it is this which the visitor enters. This area has a higher ceiling, and mediation between it and the "hypostyle" is achieved by means of an arc of glass suspended from the ceiling and etched with further clouds. These are in two layers on the glass, creating a parallax effect that is like looking up at cumulus and cirrus clouds blown along by the winds at different altitudes. The whole composition is not unlike a giant version of the Aurora lamp.

For the exhibition of their own work that

toured Europe in 1990,[5] King and Miranda constructed tableaux to comment on selected examples, adding new layers of allusion to works already laden with metaphors through their design and naming. Using mixed media – pastels, oils, acrylics, charcoal and pencil washed with various solvents for different smudging effects – the designers created large paintings to hang from or behind their products. A rendering of a burning book on the Bloom shelf system is entitled *Fireproof Alexandria*; the Vestita chair replaces a Madonna and angel in a setting borrowed from a painting by Fra Angelico. In front of the artwork is a real Vestita chair, and, in counterpoint to it, a ball with two feathers, the assemblage favoured by the Spanish painter Joan Miró to represent a female figure. More open to immediate interpretation is an Adam and Eve diptych. The interface between the two figures is a snake-like rack which offers, by way of temptation, a range of Olivetti keyboards as well as the usual apple.

Whatever the images used and the memories and thoughts they generate, the painterliness of King and Miranda's interiors is inescapable, as is the success with which the designers translate two-dimensional visions into three dimensions. "They have the ability to create very distinctive and strong interiors

La Casa del Dogon, steel, brass, video monitors and mirror. The monitors play contrasting images of the natural and designed worlds

without spending a lot of their client's money,"
notes Stephen Kiviat of Atelier International.
"Compared to another kind of solution where
there are many expensive materials and details,
they tend to do bold, simple things that are
effective in creating a strong presence."
Portoghese sees the Paris showroom in
particular slightly differently: "The space was
very difficult, and I would say that, seeing the
result, I am very pleased, but once more I feel
that there are too many good ideas – probably
two or three major ideas that could have been
used for three or four showrooms. There is a
great deal of enthusiasm and generosity – they
will never learn! They tend to confect a very
nice cage. It's so nice in itself that it doesn't
require the furniture. I need tools to show
furniture more than spaces that are interesting
in themselves."

And yet it comes as little surprise to
find King and Miranda using the same
terminology. Of their 1990 showroom for
Interdecor in Tokyo, they write that "the
showroom is not only an expression of the
image of Interdecor, it is also a tool to display
the best of modern furniture, a theatre in
which each piece can play its part and show
its qualities."[6] Though they do not say so
explicitly, there is no doubt that they regard
the Marcatré showrooms, which share many

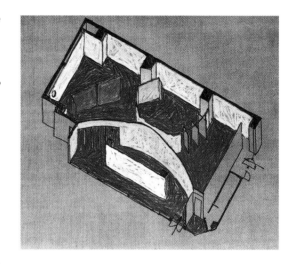

of the same characteristics, in the same light –
as tools for the display of furniture.

The strong personal flavour of King and
Miranda's showrooms has so far worked to the
benefit of Marcatré, which has in effect gained
a sophisticated and much admired corporate
identity. But now the designers face the
challenge of adapting their language for
a public interior that is not a Marcatré
showroom – the Florence showroom for
Flos/Arteluce. How they reconcile the need
to differentiate the style from that used for the
furniture company with the wish to exercise
personal expression is yet to be seen. None the
less, it is a job King and Miranda are pleased
to have won. It will be the first Flos/Arteluce

Opposite and left: King
and Miranda's Tokyo
Interdecor showroom
of 1989 has greatly
raised their profile
in Japan and has led
to an architectural
commission from
the same client

King and Miranda liken
the design of their
Tokyo Interdecor
showroom to a
landscape with
mountains traversed by
a narrow pass. Above is
a dark blue sky dotted
with stars, below a
dark, rich earth

King and Miranda
see the dramatic
arrangement of interior
space in the Tokyo
Interdecor showroom
as a tool to give impact
to the furniture display

showroom not to have been designed by Achille Castiglioni.

There is only one way to progress from designing ever grander and more elaborate interiors, and that is to graduate to full-blown architecture. Though not architects by training, King and Miranda are now taking on architectural projects. It can afford them no little satisfaction to have attained this summit by climbing, as it were, the north face without the oxygen of an Italian architectural training.

In 1986 King and Miranda designed a mixed-use building for a Tokyo construction company. The project was later scrapped but there are currently renewed prospects for a move into more ambitious architectural projects

The quality of their architecture remains to be seen, and indeed it is hard to imagine what it will be like, given the predominantly graphic handling of their interiors.

King and Miranda had begun work on their first architectural project in 1986, a small mixed-use block in Tokyo for the Rikugo Construction Company. This scheme will not now be built, but in any case it has already been eclipsed by the promise of a far larger project for a hotel complex, also in Japan. The demands of the job fit well with the way King and Miranda hope to see their business develop in the 1990s. The project will not be a one-off with a superstar signature, like Philippe Starck's Royalton Hotel in New York, but will require a major multidisciplinary commitment, drawing upon the expert knowledge of specialists in a wide range of relevant areas, notably space planning and standardised construction techniques.

The Seville Expo lighting commission was the prototype for this new mode of operation. There King and Miranda have had to draw together everyone from engineering designers at Philips Lighting, to scientists who would model the lighting proposals by computer, to production companies that could make video presentations of the project proposals. The designers see themselves in future taking on

Overleaf: The fleecy golden clouds of the Paris showroom are transformed at Interdecor in Tokyo into an improbably solid surrealistic object glimpsed through a porthole window

ever bigger projects, yet still being able to retain a large degree of design control without having greatly to expand the studio. The word they use is "ringmasters".

In addition to Seville and the Japanese hotel, there is talk of a similar co-ordinating role on a large-scale transportation project. "These sorts of project involve many more experts than we have in our organisation," says King. "But we now feel able to undertake them because we have built up a mechanism outside the studio which enables us to do this practically and easily." King talks vaguely of a network of Milan specialists in design and technical disciplines who have grown as Studio King-Miranda has grown, and of a frighteningly efficient secretarial hub that will co-ordinate the whole circus.

If this ambitious gambit pays off, it promises to unite threads of interest that have been pursued concurrently but largely separately throughout King and Miranda's career together. On the one hand, there are the rigours of the work for Olivetti, from the design of computer typefaces to speculation about the office of the future, and the understanding of the demands of technology both present and future. On the other, there is the poetic simplicity of the Arteluce lamps and the poetic complexity of the Marcatré

interiors and furniture, all laden with their own messages and quotations from our culture, past and present. It is hard to imagine a team of designers better able to marry the cultural and the technological, to draw together the past, the present and the future, into a convincing whole.

1. G. Dorfles, "King, Miranda and Design: Modern but not Post-Modern", essay for the Spanish award, El Premio Nacional de Diseño Industrial, reprinted in *Lonely Tools: Work 1976-1990*, King-Miranda Associati exhibition catalogue, 1990.
2. Notes on the Marcatré Rome showroom, King-Miranda Associati (unpublished).
3. E. M. Farrelly, "A Well-Mixed Metaphor: Shaken not Stirred", *The Architectural Review*, July 1988, pp.72-6.
4. Notes on the Marcatré London showroom, King-Miranda Associati (unpublished).
5. *Lonely Tools: Work 1976-1990, ibid.*
6. Notes on the Interdecor Tokyo showroom, King-Miranda Associati (unpublished).

"When is a Dot not a Dot?", *Design*, May 1975, p.22

"Freiraüme für Visuelle Lösungen", *Form*, No. 70, 1975

King, P. A., "Designing for Olivetti", *Typographic*, December 1982, pp.12-15

Woudhuysen, J., "Priests at Technology's Altar", *Design*, February 1983, pp.40-2

"Perry A. King and Santiago Miranda", *Space Design*, March 1983, pp.21-7

Miranda, S., "Storia di un Progetto", *Domus*, April 1983, pp.64-5

"At Last—the Sensuous Keyboard", *Design*, April 1983, pp.50-1

"Ertastete tastaturen: Taktile Informationsschriften", *Form*, No. 101, 1983

Barbacetto, G., "Il non Facile Strumento per Sedersi", *Interni Annual*, 1984, pp.10-11 (in Italian and English)

"Perry King e Santiago Miranda", *Interni Annual*, 1984, p.11 (in Italian and English)

Thackara, J., "Inspired by Dodgem Cars", *Design*, January 1984, pp.38-9

Terzi, Anna, "Santiago Miranda", *Interni*, September 1984, pp.18-19

Axis, Autumn 1984, pp.66-7

Glancey, J., "Furniture Showrooms: Rome and Milan", *The Architectural Review*, December 1984, pp.66-71

Barbacetto, G., "Tastiera per Operatore Ingenuo", *Modo*, April 1985, pp.44-7

Sudjic, D., "Perry and Santiago and Jill", *Blueprint*, April 1985, pp.14-15

Glancey, J., "High-Flier from Milan", *The Architectural Review*, May 1985, pp.53-7

"Recent Work of Perry A. King and Santiago Miranda", *Space Design*, June 1985, pp.80-3 (in Japanese)

Farrelly, E. M. "A Well-Mixed Metaphor: Shaken not Stirred", *The Architectural Review*, July 1985, pp.72-6

"Perry King, Santiago Miranda", *Ufficio Stile*, August/September 1985, pp.2-6

Viladas, P., "Sense and Sensibility",

Progressive Architecture, September 1985, pp.114-19

Manzini, E., *La Materia dell'Invenzione*, Arcadia Edizioni, Milan 1986 (*The Material of Invention*, Design Council, London 1989)

Mantica, C., "Design e Comunicazione del Prodotto", *Gap Casa*, February/March 1986, pp.60, 65

"King-Miranda Duo Dinamico", *De Diseño*, July 1986

Barbacetto, G., *Design interface. How Man and Machine Communicate. Olivetti Design Research by King and Miranda*, Arcadia Edizioni, Milan 1987

Viladas, P., "P/A Profile: King-Miranda Associates", *Progressive Architecture*, September 1987, pp.118-27

"Fashion Cycles", *Blueprint*, September 1987, pp.28-9

"Gli Uffici Cassina e Casatec a Tokio", *Abitare*, November 1987, pp.218-21 (in Italian and English)

Myerson, J., "A King in Exile", *Design Week*, 4 December 1987, pp.16-17

ON Diseño, No. 90, 1988, special issue (mostly in Spanish)

Morozzi, C., "Il Vocabolario del Design", *Modo*, February/March 1988, pp.34-7 (in Italian with English abstract)

"Cassina au Japon", *L'Architecture d'Aujourd'hui*, April 1988, pp.84-5

"Vuelta Tables", *L'Architecture d'Aujourd'hui*, April 1988, p.88

Dolce, J., "Four Designers", *International Design*, January/February 1989, pp.52-9

"Espaces Pluriels", *Techniques et Architecture*, April/May 1989, pp.160-2

"A Fresh Palette for the Office", *Blueprint*, June 1989, pp.40-3

Raimondi, S., "Sdrammatizzare il Ruolo di Designer", *Habitat Ufficio*, June/July 1989, pp.68-77

Miranda, S., "La Spagna è Sogno", *Interni*, July/August 1989, pp.2-3

"Marcatré à Paris", *L'Architecture d'Aujourd'hui*, September 1989, p.170

Myerson, J., "Redrawing the National Boundaries", *D*, Autumn 1989, pp.20-1

Raimondi, S., "Sdrammatizzare il Ruolo di Designer", *Habitat Ufficio*, October/November 1989, pp.94-9

"Ogni Anno una Parete Nuova", *Abitare*, November 1989, pp.134-9

Yagüe, E., "Santiago Miranda—El Diseño no es Cosa de Mariquitas", *Gente*, pp.34-6